Acknowledgme

MW01047383

It was really a wonderful experience writing a book on something that I love to do because the challenges I faced during this time made me scrutinise even the smallest of my mistakes and cleared my misconceptions about many things.

This has been my first project of writing a book and naturally many people got associated with it. I feel any recognition for the merit of this book should first knock on their door.

I am thankful to all the faculty members of my college to provide me with excellent knowledge and expanding my horizon to think out of the box, especially the department of CSE and IT of SRMIST NCR. I am indebted to my programming teachers for providing me with the excellent notes that came in handy while writing this book.

I am grateful to my elder sister Aanchal Narad for reviewing everything while I was working with this book. I would like to express my gratitude towards my father Mr Rakesh Narad, my mother Mrs Vandana Narad and all my family and friends for always supporting me and for driving me to move forward.

I offer special thanks to my grandparents who are no longer with me, but their belief in me has made this journey possible.

Preface

Writing a book is certainly a strenuous task and an uphill battle, but not hard enough to overpower my motivation to complete it in the best possible way. The reason why I say this is that as a student pursuing B-tech in Computer Science and Engineering at SRM Institute of Science and Technology, I began to teach few of my friends with no programming background about fundamentals of programming during lunch breaks purely out of my love for CS. During these sessions was when it first occurred to me that writing a book will help larger pool of students.

To be able to accomplish it, I had to be profound with all the concepts that were out there, so I started to dig deeper into the basics with the help of my professors and eventually got in a habit of reading related books and blogs on internet. In the process, I planned a format for the book that can help students with the theory that was in parallel with the academic syllabus of B-tech in C.S.E and 100 most hand-picked programming problems with detailed solutions to help inculcate strong foundation for coding preface and give a head start for getting into competitive coding.

This book is based on C language as it is the most fundamental programming language that is used in almost every operating system. It is a general purpose language developed by Dennis Ritchie in 1972 and since then became the most widely used programming language. It is also the first language that is taught in most of the engineering colleges in India.

I have poured in my best efforts to make this book very simplistic but at the same time the solutions to the programs are as comprehensive as possible to give essence of what actually happens during the execution of each statement. All the programs in this book were written and executed in Xcode, an Integrated Development Environment developed by Apple.

I have essentially designed this book for beginners who aspire to become great programmers in future .I hope you enjoy this book and I believe you would find it very fruitful and effective.

INDEX

PATTERN PRINTING (Total - 18 : Pg 98-118)

THEORY

IMPORTANT DEFINITIONS AND CONCEPTS

The skills of problem solving

Problem solving requires two distinct types of mental skill, analytical and creative.

Analytical or logical thinking includes skills such as ordering, comparing, contrasting, evaluating and selecting. It provides a logical framework for problem solving and helps to select the best alternative from those available by narrowing down the range of possibilities (a convergent process).. Analytical thinking often predominates in solving closed problems, where the many possible causes have to be identified and analysed to find the real cause.Creative thinking is a divergent process, using the imagination to create a large range of ideas for solutions. It requires us to look beyond the obvious, creating ideas which may, at first, seem unrealistic or have no logical connection with the problem. There is a large element of creative thinking in solving open problems.

The creative thinking skills can be divided into several key elements:
- fluency - producing many ideas
- flexibility - producing a broad range of ideas . originality - producing uncommon ideas
- elaboration - developing ideas.

Effective problem solving requires a controlled mixture of analytical and creative thinking.

Research has shown that, in general terms, each side or hemisphere of the brain is specialised to serve one of these groups of skills. The degree of specialisation of each hemisphere varies from person to person, but it has given rise to the terms right-brain thinking and left-brain thinking. Left-brain thinking is more logical and analytical, and is predominantly verbal. Right-brain thinking is more holistic and is concerned with feelings and impressionistic relationships.

To be a good problem solver you need to be able to switch from one group of skills to the other and back again, although this is not always easy. Traditional education gives far greater encouragement to the development and use of left-brain thinking. This is reinforced in the way we are required to work, where emphasis is placed on rational, logical analysis of data in drawing conclusions.

Some other terms which are often used in discussions of creativity include:

Intuition - the ability to draw conclusions based on impressions and feelings rather than hard facts. It is a characteristic of right-brain thinking and some people rely on it more than others.Incubation - the period between stopping conscious work on a problem and the time when we become aware of a solution or part solution. People struggling with problems often suddenly become aware of a solution after a period of incubation, during which the mind is occupied by other things.

Invention - the creation of new, meaningful ideas or concepts.

Innovation - putting new ideas or concepts to a practical use, as in the development of a new product or service.

List and describe the six problem-solving steps to solve a problem that has an algorithmic solution.

People make decisions every day to solve problems that affect their lives. The problems may be as unimportant as what to watch on television or as important as choosing a new profession. If a bad decision is made, time and resources are wasted, so it's important that people know how to make decisions well. There are six steps to follow to ensure the best decision. These six steps in problem solving include the following:

1. **Identify the problem.** The first step toward solving a problem is to identify the problem. In a classroom situation, most problems have been identified for you and given to you in the form of written assignments or problems out of a book.However, when you are doing problem solving outside the classroom, you need to make sure you identify the problem before you start solving it. If you don't know what the problem is, you cannot solve it.

2. **Understand the problem**. You must understand what is involved in the problem before you can continue toward the solution. This includes understanding the knowledge base of the person or machine for whom you are solving the problem. If you are setting up a solution for a person, then you must know what that person knows. A different set of instructions might have to be used depending on this knowledge base. For example, you would use a more detailed set of instructions to tell someone how to find a restaurant in your city if he has a limited knowledge of the city than if he knows it well. When you are working with a computer, its knowledge base is the limited instructions the computer can understand in the particular language or application you are using to solve the problem. Knowing the knowledge base is very important since you cannot use any instructions outside this base. You also must know your own knowledge base. You cannot solve a problem if you do not know the subject. For example, to solve a problem involving calculus, you must know calculus; to solve a problem involving accounting, you must know accounting. You must be able to communicate with your client and be able to understand what is involved in solving the problem.

3. **Identify alternative ways to solve the problem.** This list should be as complete as possible. You might want to talk to other people to find other solutions than those you have identified. Alternative solutions must be acceptable ones. You could go from Denver to Los Angeles by way of New York, but this would probably

not be an acceptable solution to your travel needs.

4. **Select the best way to solve the problem from the list of alternative solutions.** In this step, you need to identify and evaluate the pros and cons of each possible solution before selecting the best one. In order to do this, you need to select criteria for the evaluation. These criteria will serve as the guidelines for evaluating each solution.

5. **List instructions that enable you to solve the problem using the selected solution.** These numbered, step-by-step instructions must fall within the knowledge base set up in step 2. No instruction can be used unless the individual or the machine can understand it. This can be very limiting, especially when working with computers.

6. **Evaluate the solution.** To evaluate or test a solution means to check its result to see if it is correct, and to see if it satisfies the needs of the person(s) with the problem. (When a person needs a piece of furniture to sleep on, buying her a cot may be a *correct* solution, but it may not be very satisfactory.) If the result is either incorrect or unsatisfactory, then the problem solver must review the list of instructions to see that they are correct or start the process all over again.

What is Creative Thinking?

Creative thinking means thinking about new things or thinking in new ways. It is "thinking outside the box." Often, creativity in this sense involves what is called lateral thinking, or the ability to perceive patterns that are not obvious. Creative people can devise new ways to carry out tasks, solve problems, and meet challenges. They bring a fresh and sometimes unorthodox perspective to their work and can help departments and organisations to move in more productive directions.

What do you mean by an algorithm?

An **algorithm** is procedure consisting of a finite set of unambiguous rules (instructions) which specify a finite sequence of operations that provides the solution to a problem, or to a specific class of problems for any allowable set of input quantities (if there are inputs). In other word, an **algorithm** is a step-by-step procedure to solve a given problem.

What do you mean by flowcharting?

Flowcharting is a tool developed in the computer industry, for showing the steps involved in a process. A flowchart is a diagram made up of boxes, diamonds and other shapes, connected by arrows - each shape represents a step in the process, and the arrows show the order in which they occur. Flowcharting combines symbols and flow lines, to show figuratively the operation of an algorithm.

Write an algorithm to find out number is odd or even?

step 1 : start
step 2 : input number
step 3 : rem=number mod 2
step 4 : if rem=0 then
            print "number even"
        else
            print "number odd"
        endif
step 5 : stop

Describe salient features of C Language.

Industry Presence : Over the last decade C has become one of the most widely used development languages in the software industry. Its importance is not entirely derived from its use as a primary development language but also because of its use as an interface language to some of the newer "visual" languages and of course because of its relationship with C++.

Middle Level : Being a Middle level language it combines elements of high level languages with the functionality of assembly language. C supports data types and operations on data types in much the same way as higher level languages as well as allowing direct manipulation of bits, bytes, words and addresses as is possible with low level languages.

Portability : With the availability of compilers for almost all operating systems and hardware platforms it is easy to write code on one system which can be easily ported to another as long as a few simple guidelines are followed.

Flexibility : Supporting its position as the mainstream development language C can be interfaced readily to other programming languages.

Malleable : C, unlike some other languages, offers little restriction to the programmer with regard to data types -- one type may be coerced to another type as the situation dictates. However this *feature* can lead to sloppy coding unless the programmer is fully aware of what rules are being bent and why.

Speed : The availability of various optimising compilers allow extremely efficient code to be generated automatically.

Write short history of C.

The C Programming Language was initially developed by Denis Ritchie using a Unix system in 1972. This was varied and modified until a standard was defined by Brian Kernighan and Dennis Ritchie in 1978 in "The C Programming Language".

By the early 80's many versions of C were available which were inconsistent with each other in many aspects. This led to a standard being defined by ANSI in 1983. It is this standard this set of notes primarily addresses.

MACHINE LANGUAGES :

- In the earliest days of computers, the only programming languages available were machine languages.
- Each computer has its own machine language, which made of streams 0's and 1's.
- The instruction must be in streams of 0's and 1's because the internal circuits of computer are made of switches, transistors and other electronic devices.

SYMBOLIC LANGUAGES:

- Admiral Grace Hopper, a mathematician developed the concepts of a special computer (language) program that would convert programs into machine language.
- These programming languages mirrored the machine languages using symbols or mnemonics to represent various machine language instructions.
- Because of the usage of symbols they were known as Symbolic languages.
- A special program called as assembler translates symbolic code into machine language.
- Symbolic languages are also known as assembly languages as they had to be assembled into machine language.

HIGH LEVEL LANGUAGE:

- Working with symbolic languages is very tedious because each machine instruction had to be individually coded. To solve the problem and to improve programmer efficiency high level languages were developed.
- High level languages are portable to many different computers.
- However high level languages are also to be converted into machine language.
- The process of converting high level language to machine language is called "COMPILATION".

STRUCTURE OF C PROGRAM:

- Every c program contains a number of building blocks known as functions.
- Each function of it performs task independently.
- A function is a subroutine that may consist of one or more statements.
- C program comprises different sections.

The following figure depicts the structure of c program

```
Header file section

Global declaration section


/*comments*/

main()

{

Declaration part

Executable part

}

User defined functions

{

}
```

HEADER FILE SECTION OR PREPROCESSOR DIRECTIVES:

- Preprocessor commands are special instructions to the preprocessor that tell it how to prepare the program for compilation.
- The preprocessor commands appear at the beginning of the program.
- All preprocessor commands start with a pound (#) sign.
- The preprocessor command tells the compiler to include the library files within the program.
- The complete syntax of the command is: #include<stdio.h>
- The library file that must be included within the program has to be placed in between(<>)
- (.h) is the extension for all the library files included which mean that they are header files.

GOLBAL DECLARATION:

- This section declares some variables that are used in more than one function.
- These variables are known as global variables.

FUNCTION main():

- Every program written in C language must contain the main() function.
- Empty parentheses after main are necessary.
- The execution of program always being with the function main().
- The program execution starts from opening brace({) and ends with closing brace(}).

DECLARATION PART:

- The declaration part declares all variables that are used in executable part.
- Initialization of variables is also done in this section in which initial values are provided to the variable.

EXECUTABLE PART:

- This part contains the statements following the declaration of the variable.
- This part contains a set of statements or a single statement.

USER DEFINED FUNCTION:

- The functions defined by the programmer/user are called user defined functions.
- These functions are declared after the main() function.

CREATING AND RUNNING PROGRAMS:

Computer hardware understands a program only if it is coded in its machine language. It is the job of the programmer to write and test the program. There are four steps in this process. They are as follows

87. Writing and editing the program
88. Compiling the program
89. Linking the program with required library modules
90. Executing the program

Writing and editing programs:

- The software used to write programs is called "TEXT EDITOR'
- Our text editor could be a generalised word processor.
- After we complete a program. We save our file to disk.
- This saved file will be input to the compiler and it is known as " source file".

Compiling programs:

The code in a source file stored on disk must be translated in to machine language which is the job of compiler.

The C compiler is actually two separate programs (i) preprocessor (ii) translator .

- The preprocessor reads the source code and prepares it for the translator.
- While preparing the code, it scans for special instructions known as preprocessor commands.
- These commands tell the preprocessors to look for special code libraries make substitutions in the code.
- It prepares the code for translation in to machine language.
- The result of preprocessing unit is called translation unit.
- The translator does the actual process of converting the programs in to machine languages.
- The translator reads the translation unit and writes the resulting object module to a file that can then be combined with other precompiled units to form final program

- High level languages are also to be converted in to machine languages
- The process of converting high level languages to machine languages is called "compilation "

What is constant? Write down briefly about different type of constant?

- C Constants are also like normal variables. But, only difference is, their values can not be modified by the program once they are defined.
- Constants refer to fixed values. They are also called as literals
- Constants may be belonging to any of the data type.

Syntax:
const data_type variable_name; (or) const data_type *variable_name;

Types of C constant:
1. Integer constants
2. Real or Floating point constants
3. Octal & Hexadecimal constants
4. Character constants
5. String constants
6. Backslash character constants

S.no	Constant type	data type	Example
1	Integer constants	int unsigned int long int long long int	53, 762, -478 etc 5000u, 1000U etc 483,647 2,147,483,680
2	Real or Floating point constants	float doule	10.456789 600.123456789
3	Octal constant	int	013 /* starts with 0 */
4	Hexadecimal constant	int	0×90 /* starts with 0x */
5	character constants	char	'A' , 'B', 'C'
6	string constants	char	"ABCD" , "Hai"

Rules for constructing C constant:

1. *Integer Constants in C:*

   - An integer constant must have at least one digit.
   - It must not have a decimal point.
   - It can either be positive or negative.
   - No commas or blanks are allowed within an integer constant.
   - If no sign precedes an integer constant, it is assumed to be positive.
   - The allowable range for integer constants is -32768 to 32767.

2. *Real constants in C:*

   - A real constant must have at least one digit
   - It must have a decimal point
   - It could be either positive or negative
   - If no sign precedes an integer constant, it is assumed to be positive.
   - No commas or blanks are allowed within a real constant.

3. *Character and string constants in C:*

   - A character constant is a single alphabet, a single digit or a single special symbol enclosed within single quotes.
   - The maximum length of a character constant is 1 character.
   - String constants are enclosed within double quotes.

4. *Backslash Character Constants in C:*

   - There are some characters which have special meaning in C language.
   - They should be preceded by backslash symbol to make use of special function of them.
   - Given below is the list of special characters and their purpose.

How to use constants in a C program

- We can define constants in a C program in the following ways.

- By "const" keyword

- By "#define" preprocessor directive

- Please note that when you try to change constant values after defining in C program, it will through error.

What do you mean by variable?

- C variable is a named location in a memory where a program can manipulate the data. This location is used to hold the value of the variable.
- The value of the C variable may get change in the program.
- C variable might be belonging to any of the data type like int, float, char etc.

What are rules for naming C variables?

Rules for naming C variable:

1. Variable name must begin with letter or underscore.
2. Variables are case sensitive
3. They can be constructed with digits, letters.
4. No special symbols are allowed other than underscore.
5. sum, height, _value are some examples for variable name

How will you declare and initialise C Variable?

Declaring & initialising C variable:

- Variables should be declared in the C program before to use.
- Memory space is not allocated for a variable while declaration. It happens only on variable definition.
- Variable initialization means assigning a value to the variable.

S.No	Type	Syntax	Example
1	Variable declaration	data_type variable_name;	int x, y, z; char flat, ch;
2	Variable initialization	data_type variable_name = value;	int x = 50, y = 30; char flag = 'x', ch='l';

What are different types of variables in C?

There are three types of variables in C program They are,

1. Local variable
2. Global variable
3. Environment variable

Difference between variable declaration & definition in C:

S.no	Variable declaration	Variable definition
1	Declaration tells the compiler about data type and size of the variable.	Definition allocates memory for the variable.
2	Variable can be declared many times in a program.	It can happen only one time for a variable in a program.
3	The assignment of properties and identification to a variable.	Assignments of storage space to a variable.

What is a data type and name different types of data types available in c?

- C data types are defined as the data storage format that a variable can store a data to perform a specific operation.
- Data types are used to define a variable before to use in a program.
- Size of variable, constant and array are determined by data types.

C – data types:

There are four data types in C language. They are,

S.no	Types	Data Types
1	Basic data types	int, char, float, double
2	Enumeration data type	enum
3	Derived data type	pointer, array, structure, union
4	Void data type	void

1. Basic data types in C:

1.1. Integer data type:

- Integer data type allows a variable to store numeric values.
- "int" keyword is used to refer integer data type.

- The storage size of int data type is 2 or 4 or 8 byte.

- It varies depend upon the processor in the CPU that we use. If we are using 16 bit processor, 2 byte (16 bit) of memory will be allocated for int data type.

- Like wise, 4 byte (32 bit) of memory for 32 bit processor and 8 byte (64 bit) of memory for 64 bit processor is allocated for int datatype.

- int (2 byte) can store values from -32,768 to +32,767

- int (4 byte) can store values from -2,147,483,648 to +2,147,483,647.

- If you want to use the integer value that crosses the above limit, you can go for "long int" and "long long int" for which the limits are very high.

Note:

- We can't store decimal values using int data type.

- If we use int data type to store decimal values, decimal values will be truncated and we will get only whole number.

- In this case, float data type can be used to store decimal values in a variable.

1.2. Character data type:

- Character data type allows a variable to store only one character.

- Storage size of character data type is 1. We can store only one character using character data type.

- "char" keyword is used to refer character data type.

- For example, 'A' can be stored using char datatype. You can't store more than one character using char data type.

1.3. Floating point data type:

Floating point data type consists of 2 types. They are,

1. float
2. double

1. float:

- Float data type allows a variable to store decimal values.

- Storage size of float data type is 4. This also varies depend upon the processor in the CPU as "int" data type.

- We can use up-to 6 digits after decimal using float data type.

- For example, 10.456789 can be stored in a variable using float data type.

2. double:

- Double data type is also same as float data type which allows up-to 10 digits after decimal.

- The range for double datatype is from 1E–37 to 1E+37.

1.3.1. sizeof() function in C:

sizeof() function is used to find the memory space allocated for each C data types.

1.3.2. Modifiers in C:

- The amount of memory space to be allocated for a variable is derived by modifiers.
- Modifiers are prefixed with basic data types to modify (either increase or decrease) the amount of storage space allocated to a variable.
- For example, storage space for int data type is 4 byte for 32 bit processor. We can increase the range by using long int which is 8 byte. We can decrease the range by using short int which is 2 byte.

There are 5 modifiers available in C language. They are,

1. short
2. long
3. signed
4. unsigned
5. long long

- Below table gives the detail about the storage size of each C basic data type in 16 bit processor.
  Please keep in mind that storage size and range for int and float datatype will vary depend on the CPU processor (8,16, 32 and 64 bit)

S.No	C Data types	storage Size	Range
1	char	1	-127 to 127
2	int	2	-32,767 to 32,767
3	float	4	1E-37 to 1E+37 with six digits of precision
4	double	8	1E-37 to 1E+37 with ten digits of precision
5	long double	10	1E-37 to 1E+37 with ten digits of precision
6	long int	4	-2,147,483,647 to 2,147,483,647
7	short int	2	-32,767 to 32,767
8	unsigned short int	2	0 to 65,535
9	signed short int	2	-32,767 to 32,767
10	long long int	8	-(2power(63) -1) to 2(power)63 -1
11	signed long int	4	-2,147,483,647 to 2,147,483,647
12	unsigned long int	4	0 to 4,294,967,295

13	unsigned long long int	8	2(power)64 -1

2. Enumeration data type in C:

- Enumeration data type consists of named integer constants as a list.
- It start with 0 (zero) by default and value is incremented by 1 for the sequential identifiers in the list.
- Enum syntax in C:

enum identifier [optional{ enumerator-list }];

- Enum example in C:

enum month { Jan, Feb, Mar }; or
/* Jan, Feb and Mar variables will be assigned to 0, 1 and 2 respectively by default */
enum month { Jan = 1, Feb, Mar };
/* Feb and Mar variables will be assigned to 2 and 3 respectively by default */
enum month { Jan = 20, Feb, Mar };
/* Jan is assigned to 20. Feb and Mar variables will be assigned to 21 and 22 respectively by default */

- The above enum functionality can also be implemented by "#define" preprocessor directive as given below. Above enum example is same as given below.

#define Jan 20;
#define Feb 21;
#define Mar 22;

3. Derived data type in C:

- Array, pointer, structure and union are called derived data type in C language.

4. Void data type in C:

- Void is an empty data type that has no value.
- This can be used in functions and pointers.

Write a short note on C Operators and Expressions.

- The symbols which are used to perform logical and mathematical operations in a C program are called C operators.
- These C operators join individual constants and variables to form expressions.
- Operators, functions, constants and variables are combined together to form expressions.
- Consider the expression A + B * 5. where, +, * are operators, A, B are variables, 5 is constant and A + B * 5 is an expression.

TYPES OF C OPERATORS:

C language offers many types of operators. They are,

S.n	Types of	Description
1	Arithmetic_operator	These are used to perform mathematical calculations like
2	Assignment_operat	These are used to assign the values for the variables in C
3	Relational	These operators are used to compare the value of two
4	Logical operators	These operators are used to perform logical operations on
5	Bit wise operators	These operators are used to perform bit operations on given
6	Conditional	Conditional operators return one value if condition is true and
7	Increment/	These operators are used to either increase or decrease the
8	Special operators	&, *, sizeof( ) and ternary operators.

Arithmetic Operators in C:

- C Arithmetic operators are used to perform mathematical calculations like addition, subtraction, multiplication, division and modulus in C programs.

S.no	Arithmetic Operators	Operation	Example
1	+	Addition	A+B
2	-	Subtraction	A-B
3	*	multiplication	A*B
4	/	Division	A/B
5	%	Modulus	A%B

Assignment operators in C:

- In C programs, values for the variables are assigned using assignment operators.
- For example, if the value "10" is to be assigned for the variable "sum", it can be assigned as "sum = 10;"
- Other assignment operators in C language are given below.

Operators		Example	Explanation
Simple assignment operator	=	sum = 10	10 is assigned to variable sum
Compound assignment operators	+=	sum += 10	This is same as sum = sum + 10
	-=	sum -= 10	This is same as sum = sum – 10
	*=	sum *= 10	This is same as sum = sum * 10
	/+	sum /= 10	This is same as sum = sum / 10
	%=	sum %= 10	This is same as sum = sum % 10
	&=	sum&=10	This is same as sum = sum & 10
	^=	sum ^= 10	This is same as sum = sum ^ 10

Relational operators in C:

- Relational operators are used to find the relation between two variables. i.e. to compare the values of two variables in a C program.

S.no	Operators	Example	Description
1	>	x > y	x is greater than y
2	<	x < y	x is less than y
3	>=	x >= y	x is greater than or equal to y
4	<=	x <= y	x is less than or equal to y
5	==	x == y	x is equal to y
6	!=	x != y	x is not equal to y

Logical operators in C:

- These operators are used to perform logical operations on the given expressions.
- There are 3 logical operators in C language. They are, logical AND (&&), logical OR (||) and logical NOT (!).

S. no	Operators	Name	Example	Description
1	&&	logical AND	(x>5)&&(y<5)	It returns true when both conditions are true
2	||	logical OR	(x>=10)||(y>=10)	It returns true when at-least one of the condition is true
3	!	logical NOT	!((x>5)&&(y<5))	It reverses the state of the operand "((x>5) && (y<5))" If "((x>5) && (y<5))" is true, logical NOT operator makes it false

Bit wise operators in C:

- These operators are used to perform bit operations. Decimal values are converted into binary values which are the sequence of bits and bit wise operators work on these bits.
- Bit wise operators in C language are & (bitwise AND), | (bitwise OR), ~ (bitwise OR), ^ (XOR), << (left shift) and >> (right shift).

Truth table for bit wise operation Bit wise operators

x	y	x|y	x & y	x ^ y	Operator symbol	Operator name
0	0	0	0	0	&	Bitwise AND
0	1	1	0	1			Bitwise OR
1	0	1	0	1	~	Bitwise NOT
1	1	1	1	0	^	XOR
					<<	Left Shift
					>>	Right Shift

Conditional or ternary operators in C:

- Conditional operators return one value if condition is true and returns another value is condition is false.
- This operator is also called as ternary operator.

Syntax   :   (Condition? true_value: false_value);
Example :   (A > 100 ? 0 : 1);

In above example, if A is greater than 100, 0 is returned else 1 is returned. This is equal to if else conditional statements.

C – Increment/decrement Operators

- Increment operators are used to increase the value of the variable by one and decrement operators are used to decrease the value of the variable by one in C programs.

Syntax:

Increment operator: ++var_name; (or) var_name++;

Decrement operator: – -var_name; (or) var_name – -;

Example:

Increment operator : ++ i ;   i ++ ;

Decrement operator : - – i ;   i – - ;

Special Operators in C:

Below are some of special operators that C language offers.

S.no	Operators	Description
1	&	This is used to get the address of the variable. Example : &a will give address of a.
2	*	This is used as pointer to a variable. Example : * a where, * is pointer to the variable a.
3	Sizeof ()	This gives the size of the variable. Example : size of (char) will give us 1.

Write a short note on C – printf and scanf

printf() and scanf() functions are inbuilt library functions in C which are available in C library by default. These functions are declared and related macros are defined in "stdio.h" which is a header file.

- We have to include "stdio.h" file as shown in below C program to make use of these printf() and scanf() library functions.

1. C printf() function:

- printf() function is used to print the "character, string, float, integer, octal and hexadecimal values" onto the output screen.
- We use printf() function with %d format specifier to display the value of an integer variable.
- Similarly %c is used to display character, %f for float variable, %s for string variable, %lf for double and %x for hexadecimal variable.
- To generate a newline, we use "\n" in C printf() statement.

2. C scanf() function:

- scanf() function is used to read character, string, numeric data from keyboard
- Consider below example program where user enters a character. This value is assigned to the variable "ch" and then displayed.
- Then, user enters a string and this value is assigned to the variable "str" and then displayed.

C tokens:

- C tokens are the basic buildings blocks in C language which are constructed together to write a C program.
- Each and every smallest individual units in a C program are known as C tokens.
- C tokens are of six types. They are,
    1. Keywords   (eg: int, while),
    2. Identifiers   (eg: main, total),
    3. Constants   (eg: 10, 20),
    4. Strings   (eg: "total", "hello"),
    5. Special symbols   (eg: (), {}),
    6. Operators   (eg: +, /,-,*)

Identifiers in C language:

- Each program elements in a C program are given a name called identifiers.
- Names given to identify Variables, functions and arrays are examples for identifiers. eg. x is a name given to integer variable in above program.

Rules for constructing identifier name in C:

1. First character should be an alphabet or underscore.
2. Succeeding characters might be digits or letter.

3. Punctuation and special characters aren't allowed except underscore.
4. Identifiers should not be keywords.

Keywords in C language:

- Keywords are pre-defined words in a C compiler.
- Each keyword is meant to perform a specific function in a C program.
- Since keywords are referred names for compiler, they can't be used as variable name.

C language supports 32 keywords which are given below.

auto	double	int	struct	const	float	short	unsigned
break	else	long	switch	continue	for	signe d	void
case	enum	register	typedef	default	goto	sizeof	volatile
char	extern	return	union	do	if	static	while

Decision Making And Branching

'**C**' language processes decision making capabilities supports the flowing statements known as control or decision making statements

1. If statement
2. switch statement
3. conditional operator statement
4. Goto statement

If Statement : The if statement is powerful decision making statement and is used to control the flow of execution of statements The If statement may be complexity of conditions to be tested

(a) Simple if statement
(b) If else statement
(c) Nested If-else statement
(d) Else –If ladder

Simple If Statement : The general form of simple if statement is

             If(test expression)
{   statement block;
          }   statement-x ;

The statement -block may be a single statement or a group of statement if the test expression is true the statement block will be executed. Otherwise the statement -block will be skipped and the execution will jump to the statement –X. If the condition is true both the statement –block sequence .

Flow chart :

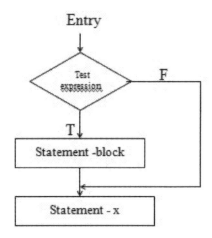

If –Else Statement : The If statement is an extension of the simple If statement the general form is

```
If (test expression)
{
    true-block statements;
}
else
{
    false-block statements;
}
statement – x;
```

If the test expression is true then block statement are executed, otherwise the false –block statement are executed. In both cases either true-block or false-block will be executed not both.

Flow chart :

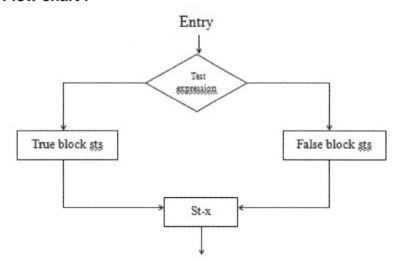

Nested If –else statement : When a series of decisions are involved we may have to use more than one if-else statement in nested form of follows .

```
 if(test expression)
{ if(test expression)
{   st –1;
}
else
{  st – 2;
}else
{
   st – 3;
}
}st – x;
```

Else-If ladder : A multi path decision is charm of its in which the statement associated with each else is an If. It takes the following general form.

Switch Statement: Instead of else –if ladder, 'C' has a built-in multi-way decision statement known as a switch. The general form of the switch statement is as follows.

```
 Switch (expression)
{
case value1   : block1;
                break;
case value 2  : block 2;
                break;
default        : default block;
                break;
}
st – x;
```

Ex :   switch (number)
```
{
case 1 : printf("Monday");
        break;
case 2 : printf("Tuesday");
        break;
case 3 : printf("Wednesday");
        break;
case 4 : printf("Thursday");
        break;
case 5 : printf("Friday");
        break;
      default : printf("Saturday");
        break;
}
```

The Conditional (? :) Operator : These operator is a combinations of question and colon and takes three operands this is also known as conditional operator. The general form of the conditional operator is as follows

Conditional expression? Expression 1:expression2

The conditional expression is evaluated first If the result is non-zero expression is evaluated and is returns as the value of the conditional expression, Otherwise expression2 is evaluated and its value is returned.

Goto Statement : The goto statement is used to transfer the control of the program from one point to another. It is something referred to as unconditionally branching. The goto is used in the form
Goto label;

Label statement : The label is a valid 'C' identifier followed by a colon. we can precode any statement by a label in the form
Label : statement

Explain C – Loop control statements in detail.

Loop control statements in C are used to perform looping operations until the given condition is true. Control comes out of the loop statements once condition becomes false.

Types of loop control statements in C:

There are 3 types of loop control statements in C language. They are,

   1. for

   2. while

   3. do-while

Syntax for each C loop control statements are given in below table with description.

S.no	Loop Name	Syntax	Description
1	for	for (exp1; exp2; expr3) { statements; }	Where, exp1 – variable initialization (Example: i=0, j=2, k=3) exp2 – condition checking (Example: i>5, j<3, k=3) exp3 – increment/decrement (Example: ++i, j–, ++k)
2	while	while (condition) { statements; }	where, condition might be a>5, i<10
3	do while	do { statements; } while (condition);	where, condition might be a>5, i<10

Difference between while & do while loops in C:

S.no	while	do while
1	Loop is executed only when condition is true.	Loop is executed for first time irrespective of the condition. After executing while loop for first time, then condition is checked.

DEFINiTION OF A FUNCTION

A function is a self- contained block of executable code that can be called from any other function . When a function is called, the control transfers to the called function, which will be executed, and then transfers the control back to the calling function (to the statement following the function call).

Program to illustrate a function

```
#include <stdio.h>
main ()
{

void sample( );
printf("\n You are in main");
}
void sample( )
{
printf("\n You are in sample"); }
```

OUTPUT

You are in sample

You are in main

The syntax of a function is:

return data type function_name (list of arguments)

```
{ datatype declaration of the arguments;
   executable statements;

   return (expression);
}
```
where,
• Return data type is the same as the data type of the variable that is returned by the function using return statement.
• A function_name is formed in the same way as variable names / identifiers are formed.

- The list of arguments or parameters are valid variable names as shown below, separated by commas: (data type1 var1, data type2 var2,........ data type n var n) for example (int x, float y, char z).

    • arguments give the values which are passed from the calling function.

    • the body of function contains executable statements.

- the return statement returns a single value to the calling function.

DECLARATION OF A FUNCTION

As we have mentioned in the previous section, every function has its declaration and function definition. When we talk of declaration only, it means only the function name, its argument list and return type are specified and the function body or definition is not attached to it. The syntax of a function declaration is:

return data type function_name(list of arguments);

For example,
int square(int no);
float temperature(float c, float f);

FUNCTION PROTOTYPES

Function Prototypes require that every function which is to be accessed should be declared in the calling function.

•Function prototype requires that the function declaration must include the return type of function as well as the type and number of arguments or parameters passed.

• The variable names of arguments need not be declared in prototype.
• The major reason to use this concept is that they enable the compiler to check if there is any mismatch between function declaration and function call.

THE RETURN STATEMENT

If a function has to return a value to the calling function, it is done through the return statement. It may be possible that a function does not return any value; only the control is transferred to the calling function. The syntax for the return statement is:

return (expression);

Points to remember:
• You can pass any number of arguments to a function but can return only one value at a time.
• If a function does not return anything, void specifier is used in the function declaration.

void square (int no)

30

```
{
int sq;
sq = no*no;

printf ("square is %d", sq);

}
```

• All the function's return type is by default is "int", i.e. a function returns an integer value, if no type specifier is used in the function declaration.
Some examples are:
(i) square (int no); /* will return an integer value */

(ii) int square (int no); /* will return an integer value */ (iii) void square (int no); /* will not return anything */

 A function can have many return statements. This thing happens when some condition based returns are required.

For example,
```
/*Function to find greater of two numbers*/ int greater (int x, int y)
{
if (x>y)
return (x);
else
return (y);

}
```

Scope, visibility of variables in functions

In a program consisting of a number of functions a number of different types of variables can be found.
Global vs. Local variables: Global variables are recognised through out the program whereas local valuables are recognised only within the function where they are defined.

Static vs. Dynamic variables: Retention of value by a local variable means, that in static, retention of the variable value is lost once the function is completely executed whereas in certain conditions the value of the variable has to be retained from the earlier execution and the execution retained.

The variables can be characterised by their data type and by their storage class. One way to classify a variable is according to its data type and the other can be through its storage class. Data type refers to the type of value represented by a variable whereas storage class refers to the permanence of a variable and its scope within the program i.e. portion of the program over which variable is recognised.

Storage Classes

There are four different storage classes specified in C:
1. Automatic 2. External 3. Static 4. Register

TYPES OF FUNCTION INVOKING

We categorize a function's invoking (calling) depending on arguments or parameters and their returning a value.
The various types of invoking functions are:

• With no arguments and with no return value.

• With no arguments and with return value

• With arguments and with no return value

• With arguments and with return value.

TYPE 1: With no arguments and have no return value

As the name suggests, any function which has no arguments and does not return any values to the calling function, falls in this category. These type of functions are confined to themselves i.e. neither do they receive any data from the calling function nor do they transfer any data to the calling function. So there is no data communication between the calling and the called function are only program control will be transferred.
/* Program for illustration of the function with no arguments and no return value*/
/* Function with no arguments and no return value*/

```
#include <stdio.h>
main()
{
void message();
printf("Control is in main\n");
message(); /* Type 1 Function */
printf("Control is again in main\n");
}
void message()
{
printf("Control is in message function\n");
} /* does not return anything */
```

OUTPUT
Control is in main
Control is in message function
Control is again in main

TYPE 2: With no arguments and with return value

Suppose if a function does not receive any data from calling function but does send some value to the calling function, then it falls in this category.

Write a program to find the sum of the first ten natural numbers. /* Program to find sum of first ten natural numbers */

```
#include <stdio.h>
int cal_sum()

{
int i, s=0;
for (i=0; i<=10; i++)
s=s + i;
return(s); /* function returning sum of first ten natural numbers */ }

main()
{
int sum;
sum = cal_sum();
printf("Sum of first ten natural numbers is % d\n", sum); }
```

OUTPUT

Sum of first ten natural numbers is 55

TYPE 3: With Arguments and have no return value

If a function includes arguments but does not return anything, it falls in this category. One way communication takes place between the calling and the called function.
Before proceeding further, first we discuss the type of arguments or parameters here. There are two types of arguments:

• Actual arguments • Formal arguments

Let us take an example to make this concept clear:

Write a program to calculate sum of any three given numbers.

```
#include <stdio.h>
main()
{

int a1, a2, a3;
void sum(int, int, int);
printf("Enter three numbers: ");
scanf ("%d%d%d",&a1,&a2,&a3);
sum (a1,a2,a3); /* Type 3 function */
}
/* function to calculate sum of three numbers */
void sum (int f1, int f2, int f3)
{
int s;
s = f1+ f2+ f3;
printf ("\nThe sum of the three numbers is %d\n",s);
}
```
OUTPUT
Enter three numbers: 23 34 45
The sum of the three numbers is 102

Here f1, f2, f3 are formal arguments and a1, a2, a3 are actual arguments.
Thus we see in the function declaration, the arguments are formal arguments, but when values are passed to the function during function call, they are actual arguments.

TYPE 4: With arguments function and with return value

In this category two-way communication takes place between the calling and called function i.e. a function returns a value and also arguments are passed to it.

Write a program to calculate sum of three numbers. /*Program to calculate the sum of three numbers*/ #include <stdio.h>
main ( )

```
{
int a1, a2, a3, result;
int sum(int, int, int);
printf("Please enter any 3 numbers:\n");
scanf ("%d %d %d", & a1, &a2, &a3);
result = sum (a1,a2,a3); /* function call */
printf ("Sum of the given numbers is : %d\n", result); }
/* Function to calculate the sum of three numbers */

int sum (int f1, int f2, int f3)
{
return(f1+ f2 + f3); /* function returns a value */
}
```

OUTPUT
Please enter any 3 numbers:
34 5
Sum of the given numbers is: 12

CALL BY VALUE

Write a program to multiply the two given numbers #include <stdio.h>
main()
{

```
int x, y, z;
int mul(int, int);
printf ("Enter two numbers: \n");
scanf ("%d %d",&x,&y);
z= mul(x, y); /* function call by value */
printf ("\n The product of the two numbers is : %d", z); }

/* Function to multiply two numbers */ int mul(int a, int b)
{
int c;

c =a*b;
return(c);
```

}

OUTPUT
Enter two numbers: 23 2

The product of two numbers is: 46

Now let us see what happens to the actual and formal arguments in memory.

main( ) function   mul( )   function

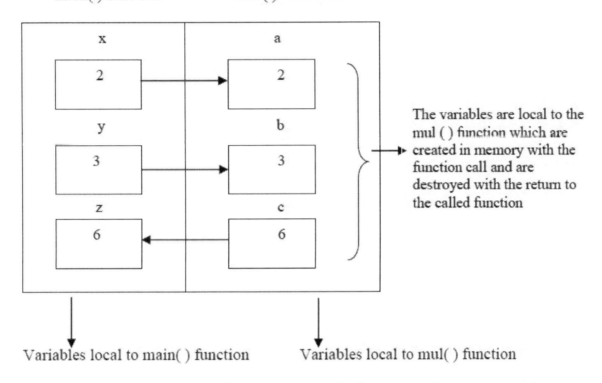

The variables are local to the mul ( ) function which are created in memory with the function call and are destroyed with the return to the called function

Variables local to main( ) function   Variables local to mul( ) function

What are meant by local variables? The answer is *local variables are those which can be used only by that function.*

Advantages of Call by value:

The only advantage is that this mechanism is simple and it reduces confusion and

complexity.

Disadvantages of Call by value:

As you have seen in the above example, there is separate memory allocation for each of

the variable, so unnecessary utilization of memory takes place.
The second disadvantage, which is very important from programming point of view, is that any changes made in the arguments are not reflected to the calling function, as these arguments are local to the called function and are destroyed with function return.

```
#include <stdio.h>
main ( )
{
int x = 2, y = 3;
```

```
void swap(int, int);
printf ("\n Values before swapping are %d %d", x, y); swap (x, y);

printf ("\n Values after swapping are %d %d", x, y); }
/* Function to swap(interchange) two values */
void swap( int a, int b )

{
int t;
t = a;
a = b;
b = t;
}
```
OUTPUT
Values before swap are 2 3 Values after swap are 2 3

But the output should have been 3   2. So what happened?

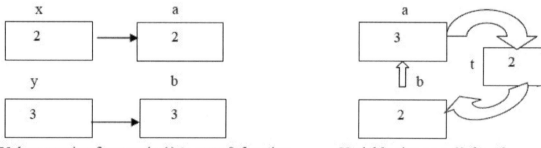

Values passing from main ( ) to swap() function   Variables in swap ( ) function

Here we observe that the changes which takes place in argument variables are not reflected in the main() function; as these variables namely a, b and t will be destroyed with function return.

RECURSION

Within a function body, if the function calls itself, the mechanism is known as 'Recursion' and the function is known as 'Recursive function'.

Write a program to find factorial of a number

/*Program to find factorial using recursion*/

```
#include<stdio.h> main()
{
int n, factorial;

int fact(int);
printf("Enter any number: \n" );

scanf("%d",&n);
factorial = fact(n); /*Function call */
```

```
printf ("Factorial is %d\n", factorial); } /* Recursive function of factorial */

int fact(int n)
{
int res;
if(n == 1) /* Terminating condition */ return(1);
else
res = n*fact(n-1); /* Recursive call */

return(res); }
```

How it works?

Suppose we will call this function with n = 5

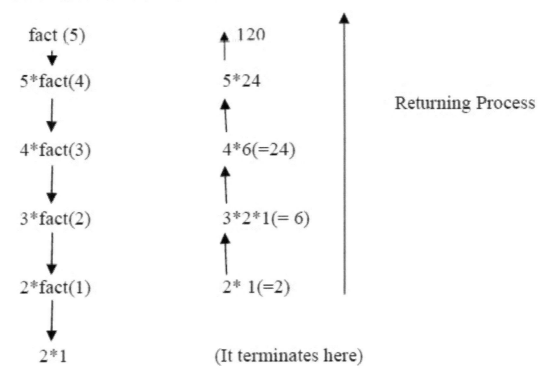

ARRAYS:

Array is a continuous memory allocation of similar data types.

Syntax of array declaration is as follows: data-type array_name [constant-size];

There are two restrictions for using arrays in C:
• The amount of storage for a declared array has to be specified at compile time before execution. This means that an array has a fixed size.
• The data type of an array applies uniformly to all the elements; for this reason, an array is called a homogeneous data structure.

37

Initialization of Array Elements in the Declaration

The values are assigned to individual array elements enclosed within the braces and separated by comma. Syntax of array initialization is as follows:
data type array-name [size] = {val 1, val 2, ...val n};
val 1 is the value for the first array element, val 2 is the value for the second element, and val n is the value for the n array element. Note that when you are initialising the values at the time of declaration, then there is no need to specify the size. Let us see some of the examples given below:

int digits [10] = {1,2,3,4,5,6,7,8,9,10};
int digits[ ] = {1,2,3,4,5,6,7,8,9,10};
int vector[5] = {12,-2,33,21,13};
float temperature[10] ={ 31.2, 22.3, 41.4, 33.2, 23.3, 32.3, 41.1, 10.8, 11.3, 42.3};

Character Array Initialization

The array of characters is implemented as strings in C. Strings are handled differently as far as initialization is concerned. A special character called null character ' \0 ', implicitly suffixes every string.

char thing [3] = "TIN";
char thing [ ] = "TIN";
In the above two statements the assignments are done differently. The first statement is not a string but simply an array storing three characters 'T', 'I' and 'N' and is same as writing:

char thing [3] = {'T', 'I', 'N'};
whereas, the second one is a four character string TIN\0. The change in the first assignment, as given below, can make it a string.
char thing [4] = "TIN";

/* Program to find the maximum marks among the marks of 10 students*/
include < stdio.h >

# define SIZE 10 /* SIZE is a symbolic constant */ main ( )
{
int i = 0;

int max = 0;
int stud_marks[SIZE]; /* array declaration */

/* enter the values of the elements */

```
for( i = 0;i<SIZE;i++)
{
printf ("Student no. =%d",i+1);

printf(" Enter the marks out of 50:");

scanf("%d",&stud_marks[i]);

} /* find maximum */
for (i=0;i<SIZE;i ++)
{
if (stud_marks[i]>max)
max = stud_marks[ i ];
}
printf("\n\nThe maximum of the marks obtained among all the 10 students is: %d
",max);
}
```

MULTI-DIMENSIONAL ARRAYS

You can declare an array of two dimensions as follows:

datatype array_name[size1][size2];
In the above example, variable_type is the name of some type of variable, such as int.
Also, size1 and size2 are the sizes of the array's first and second dimensions, respectively.

Initialization of Two - Dimensional Arrays

int table [2] [3] = { 1,2,3,4,5,6 }; It means that element
table [0][0] = 1;
table [0][1] = 2;

table [0][2] = 3; table [1][0] = 4; table [1][1] = 5; table [1][2] = 6;

The neutral order in which the initial values are assigned can be altered by including the groups in { } inside main enclosing brackets, like the following initialization as above:

int table [2] [3] = { {1,2,3}, {4,5,6} }; int table [2] [3] = { { 1, 2, 3},{ 4}};
It assigns values as
table [0][0] = 1;
table [0][1] = 2;
table [0][2] = 3;
table [1][0] = 4;
table [1][1] = 0;

table [1][2] = 0

STRINGS

String can be represented as a single-dimensional character type array

DECLARATION AND INITIALIZATION OF STRINGS

Strings in C are group of characters, digits, and symbols enclosed in quotation marks or simply we can say the string is declared as a "character array". The end of the string is marked with a special character, the '\0' (Null character), which has the decimal value 0. There is a difference between a character stored in memory and a single character string stored in a memory. The character requires only one byte whereas the single character string requires two bytes (one byte for the character and other byte for the delimiter).

Declaration of strings

A string in C is simply a sequence of characters. To declare a string, specify the data type as char and place the number of characters in the array in square brackets after the string name. The syntax is shown as below:

char string-name[size];

For example, char name[20]; char address[25]; char city[15];

Initialization of strings

The string can be initialized as follows:

char name[8] = {'P', 'R', 'O', 'G', 'R', 'A', 'M', '\0'};
Each character of string occupies 1 byte of memory (on 16 bit computing). The size of character is machine dependent, and varies from 16 bit computers to 64 bit computers.

char str[4] = {'u', 'n', 'i', 'x'}; char str[5] = {'u', 'n', 'i', 'x', '\0'}; char str[3];
char str[ ] = "UNIX";
char str[4] = "unix";
char str[9] = "unix";

All of the above declarations are legal. But which ones don't work? The first one is a valid declaration, but will cause major problems because it is not null-terminated. The second example shows a correct null-terminated string. The special escape character \0 denotes string termination. The fifth example suffers the size problem, the character array 'str' is of size 4 bytes, but it requires an additional space to store '\0'. The fourth example however does not. This is because the compiler will determine the length of the string and automatically initialize the last character to a null-terminator. The strings not terminated by a '\0' are merely a collection of characters and are called as character arrays.

40

BUILT IN STRING FUNCTIONS

The header file <string.h> contains some string manipulation functions. The following is a list of the common string managing functions in C.

Strlen Function

The strlen function returns the length of a string. It takes the string name as argument. The syntax is as follows:

n = strlen (str);

where str is name of the string and n is the length of the string, returned by strlen function.

/* Program to illustrate the strlen function to determine the length of a string */

```
#include <stdio.h>
#include <string.h>
main()

{
char name[80];
int length;
printf("Enter your name: ");
gets(name);
length = strlen(name);
printf("Your name has %d characters\n", length); }
```

Strcpy Function

The strcpy function is used to copy one string to another. The syntax is as follows:

strcpy(str1, str2);

where str1, str2 are two strings. The content of string str2 is copied on to string str1.

Write a program to read a string from the keyboard and copy the string onto the second string and display the strings on to the monitor by using strcpy( ) function.

/* Program to illustrate strcpy function*/

```
#include <stdio.h>
#include <string.h>
main()

{
char first[80], second[80];
printf("Enter a string: ");
```

```
gets(first);
strcpy(second, first);
printf("\n First string is : %s, and second string is: %s\n", first, second); }
```

Strcmp Function

The strcmp function in the string library function which compares two strings, character by character and stops comparison when there is a difference in the ASCII value or the end of any one string and returns ASCII difference of the characters that is integer. If the return value zero means the two strings are equal, a negative value means that first is less than second, and a positive value means first is greater than second. The syntax is as follows:

```
n = strcmp(str1, str2);
```
where str1 and str2 are two strings to be compared and n is returned value of differed characters.

/* The following program uses the strcmp function to compare two strings. */
```
#include <stdio.h>
#include <string.h>
main()
{
char first[80], second[80];
int value;
printf("Enter a string: ");
gets(first);
printf("Enter another string: ");
gets(second);
value = strcmp(first,second);
if(value == 0)
puts("The two strings are equal");
else if(value < 0)
puts("The first string is smaller ");
else if(value > 0)
puts("the first string is bigger");
}
```
OUTPUT
Enter a string: MOND
Enter another string: MOHANT
The first string is smaller

Strcat Function
The strcat function is used to join one string to another. It takes two strings as arguments;

the characters of the second string will be appended to the first string. The syntax is as follows: strcat(str1, str2);

where str1 and str2 are two string arguments, string str2 is appended to string str1.

Write a program to read two strings and append the second string to the first string.

/* Program for string concatenation*/

```
#include <stdio.h>
#include <string.h>
main()
{
char first[80], second[80];
printf("Enter a string:");
gets(first);
printf("Enter another string: ");
gets(second);
strcat(first, second);
printf("\nThe two strings joined together: %s\n", first);
}
```

Strlwr Function

The strlwr function converts upper case characters of string to lower case characters. The syntax is as follows:

```
strlwr(str1);
```
where str1 is string to be converted into lower case characters.

Write a program to convert the string into lower case characters using in-built function.

/* Program that converts input string to lower case characters */

```
#include <stdio.h>
#include <string.h>
main()

{
char first[80];
printf("Enter a string: ");
gets(first);
printf("Lower case of the string is %s", strlwr(first)); }
```
OUTPUT

Enter a string: BROOKES
Lower case of the string is brookes

Strrev Function

The strrev funtion reverses the given string. The syntax is as follows:

strrev(str);
where string str will be reversed.

/* Program to reverse a given string */

```
#include <stdio.h>
#include <string.h>
main()

{
char first[80];
printf("Enter a string:");
gets(first);
printf("\n Reverse of the given string is : %s ", strrev(first)); }
```

Strspn Function

The strspn function returns the position of the string, where first string mismatches with second string. The syntax is as follows:

n = strspn (first, second);
where first and second are two strings to be compared, n is the number of character from which first string does not match with second string.

/*Program which returns the position of the string from where first string does not match with second string*/

```
#include <stdio.h>
#include <string.h>

main()

{

char first[80], second[80]; printf("Enter first string: "); gets(first);
printf("\n Enter second string: "); gets(second);

printf("\n After %d characters there is no match",strspn(first, second));

}
```

OUTPUT

Enter first string: ALEXANDER Enter second string: ALEXSMITH After 4 characters there is no match

strncpy function

The strncpy function same as strcpy. It copies characters of one string to another string up to the specified length. The syntax is as follows:
strncpy(str1, str2, 10);
where str1 and str2 are two strings. The 10 characters of string str2 are copied onto string str1.

stricmp function

The stricmp function is same as strcmp, except it compares two strings ignoring the case (lower and upper case). The syntax is as follows:
n = stricmp(str1, str2);

strncmp function

The strncmp function is same as strcmp, except it compares two strings up to a specified length. The syntax is as follows:

n = strncmp(str1, str2, 10);
where 10 characters of str1 and str2 are compared and n is returned value of differed characters.

strchr function

The strchr funtion takes two arguments (the string and the character whose address is to be specified) and returns the address of first occurrence of the character in the given string. The syntax is as follows:

cp = strchr (str, c);
where str is string and c is character and cp is character pointer. strset function

The **strset funtion** replaces the string with the given character. It takes two arguments the string and the character. The syntax is as follows:

strset (first, ch);
where string first will be replaced by character ch.

STRUCTURES AND UNIONS

Structure is commonly referred to as a user-defined data type. C's structures allow you to store multiple variables of any type in one place (the structure). A structure can contain any of C's data types, including arrays and other structures. Each variable within a structure is called a member of the structure.

DECLARATION OF STRUCTURES

To declare a structure you must start with the keyword struct followed by the structure name or structure tag and within the braces the list of the structure's member variables. Note that the structure declaration does not actually create any variables. The syntax for the structure declaration is as follows:

struct structure-tag { datatype variable1; datatype variable2; dataype variable 3; ...

};

struct student {
int roll_no;
char name[20];
char course[20];
int marks_obtained ; };

The point you need to remember is that, till this time no memory is allocated to the structure. This is only the definition of structure that tells us that there exists a user-defined data type by the name of student which is composed of the following members. Using this structure type, we have to create the structure variables:

struct student stud1, stud2 ;

The second method is as follows:

struct {
int roll_no;
char name[20];

char course[20];
int marks_obtained ;

} stud1, stud2 ;

```
typedef struct country{ char name[20];
```

```
int population;
char language[10]; } Country;
```
This defines a structure which can be referred to either as struct country or Country, whichever you prefer.

INITIALIZING STRUCTURES

```
struct sale {
char customer[20];
char item[20];

float amt;
} mysale = { "XYZ Industries", "toolskit", 600.00 };

struct customer { char firm[20]; char contact[25]; }

struct sale {
struct customer buyer1;
char item [20];
float amt;
} mysale = {
{ "XYZ Industries", "Tyran Adams"}, "toolskit",
600.00
};
```

STRUCTURES AND ARRAYS

/*Program to read and print data related to five students having marks of three subjects each using the concept of arrays */

```
#include<stdio.h>
struct student {

int roll_no;
char name [20];
char course [20];
int subject [3] ;
};
main( )
{
```

47

```
struct student stud[5];
int i,j;
printf ("Enter the data for all the students:\n");
for (i=0;i<=4;i++)
{printf ("Enter the roll number of %d student",i+1);
scanf ("%d",&stud[i].roll_no);
printf("Enter the name of %d student",i+1);
scanf ("%s",stud[i].name);
printf ("Enter the course of %d student",i+1);
scanf ("%s",stud[i].course);
for (j=0;j<=2;j++)
{
printf ("Enter the marks of the %d subject of the student %d:\n",j+1,i+1); scanf
("%d",&stud[i].subject[j]);
}
}
printf ("The data you have entered is as follows:\n");
for (i=0;i<=4;i++)
{
printf ("The %d th student's roll number is %d\n",i+1,stud[i].roll_no); printf ("The %d the
student's name is %s\n",i+1,stud[i].name);
printf ("The %d the student's course is %s\n",i+1,stud[i].course);

for (j=0;j<=2;j++)
{
printf ("The %d the student's marks of %d I subject are %d\n",i+1, j+1, stud[i].subject[j]); }
}
printf ("End of the program\n");
}
```

UNIONS

Structures are a way of grouping homogeneous data together. But it often happens that at any time we require only one of the member's data. For example, in case of the support price of shares you require only the latest quotations. And only the ones that have changed need to be stored. So if we declare a structure for all the scripts, it will only lead to crowding of the memory space. Hence it is beneficial if we allocate space to only one of the members. This is achieved with the concepts of the UNIONS. UNIONS are similar to STRUCTURES in all respects but differ in the concept of storage space.

union union-tag { datatype variable1; datatype variable2; ... };

Difference Between Structure and Union:

There is an important difference in accessing the union members. Only one union member should be accessed at a time. Because a union stores its members on top of each other, it's important to access only one member at a time. Trying to access the previously stored values will result in erroneous output.

How can you access memory location of a variable?

Every variable is a memory location and every memory location has its address defined which can be accessed using ampersand &operator, which denotes an address in memory. Consider the following example, which will print the address of the variables defined:

```
#include <stdio.h>
int main()
{
int var1;
char var2[10];
printf("Address of var1 variable: %x\n", &var1 );
printf("Address of var2 variable: %x\n", &var2 );
return 0;
}
```

When the above code is compiled and executed, it produces result something as follows:

```
Address of var1 variable: bff5a400
Address of var2 variable: bff5a3f6
```

So you understood what is memory address and how to access it, so base of the concept is over.

What Are Pointers?

A **pointer** is a variable whose value is the address of another variable, i.e., direct address of the memory location. Like any variable or constant, you must declare a pointer before you can use it to store any variable address. The general form of a pointer variable declaration is:
type * var-nam e;
Here, **type** is the pointer's base type; it must be a valid C data type and **var-name** is the name of the pointer variable. The asterisk * you used to declare a pointer is the same asterisk that you use for multiplication. However, in this statement the asterisk is being used to designate a variable as a pointer. Following are the valid pointer declaration:

```
int* ip; /* pointer to an integer * /
double * dp; /* pointer to a double * /
float * fp; /* pointer to a float * /
```

char * ch/* pointer to a character * /

The actual data type of the value of all pointers, whether integer, float, character, or otherwise, is the same, a long hexadecimal number that represents a memory address. The only difference between pointers of different data types is the data type of the variable or constant that the pointer points to.

What are the benefits of using pointers?

- Pointers are more efficient in handling Array and Structure.
- Pointer allows references to function and thereby helps in passing of function as arguments to other function.
- It reduces length and the program execution time.
- It allows C to support dynamic memory management.

How Pointer variables are used in C?

There are a few important operations, which we will do with the help of pointers very frequently. **(a)** We define a pointer variable, **(b)** assign the address of a variable to a pointer and **(c)** finally access the value at the address available in the pointer variable. This is done by using unary operator * that returns the value of the variable located at the address specified by its operand. The following example makes use of these operations –

```
#include<stdio.h>
int main (){
int var=20;                                    /* actual variable declaration */
int*ip;                                        /* pointer variable declaration */
ip=&var;                                       /* store address of var in pointer variable*/
printf("Address of var variable: %x\n",&var);    /* address stored in pointer variable */
printf("Address stored in ip variable: %x\n",ip); /* access the value using the pointer */
printf("Value of *ip variable: %d\n",*ip);
return0;
}
```

OUTPUT:
Address of var variable: bffd8b3c
Address stored in ip variable: bffd8b3c
Value of *ip variable: 20

Concept of Pointer:

Whenever a variable is declared, system will allocate a location to that variable in the memory, to hold value. This location will have its own address number.
Let us assume that system has allocated memory location 80F for a variable a.
int a = 10 ;

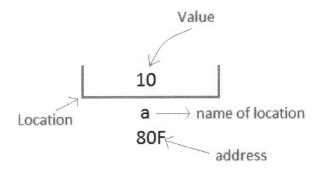

We can access the value 10 by either using the variable name a or the address 80F. Since the memory addresses are simply numbers they can be assigned to some other variable. The variable that holds memory address are called pointer variables. A pointer variable is therefore nothing but a variable that contains an address, which is a location of another variable. Value of pointer variable will be stored in another memory location.

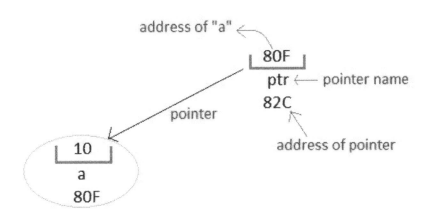

Declaring a pointer variable
General syntax of pointer declaration is,
data-type*pointer_name;
Data type of pointer must be same as the variable, which the pointer is pointing. void type pointer works with all data types, but isn't used oftenly.

Initialization of Pointer variable
Pointer Initialization is the process of assigning address of a variable to pointer variable. Pointer variable contains address of variable of same data type. In C language address operator & is used to determine the address of a variable. The & (immediately preceding a variable name) returns the address of the variable associated with it.
int a = 10 ;
int *ptr ;*//pointer declaration*
ptr = &a ;*//pointer initialization*
or,
int *ptr = &a ;*//initialization and declaration together*
Pointer variable always points to same type of data.
float a;
int *ptr;
ptr = &a;   //ERROR, type mismatch

Dereferencing of Pointer

Once a pointer has been assigned the address of a variable. To access the value of variable, pointer is dereferenced, using the indirection operator *.
inta,*p;
a = 10;
p = &a;

printf("%d",*p);   //this will print the value of a.

printf("%d",*&a); //this will also print the value of a.

printf("%u",&a); //this will print the address of a.

printf("%u",p); //this will also print the address of a.

printf("%u",&p); //this will also print the address of p.

Define NULL Pointers

It is always a good practice to assign a NULL value to a pointer variable in case you do not have an exact address to be assigned. This is done at the time of variable declaration. A pointer that is assigned NULL is called a null pointer.
The NULL pointer is a constant with a value of zero defined in several standard libraries. Consider the following program –

```
#include<stdio.h>
int main ()
{
int*ptr= NULL;
printf("The value of ptr is : %x\n",ptr);
return0;
}
```

OUTPUT:
The value of ptr is 0

Explain pointer arithmetic in detail.

A pointer in c is an address, which is a numeric value. Therefore, you can perform arithmetic operations on a pointer just as you can on a numeric value. There are four arithmetic operators that can be used on pointers: ++, --, +, and -
To understand pointer arithmetic, let us consider that **ptr** is an integer pointer which points to the address 1000. Assuming 32-bit integers, let us perform the following arithmetic operation on the pointer –
ptr++
After the above operation, the **ptr** will point to the location 1004 because each time ptr is incremented, it will point to the next integer location which is 4 bytes next to the current

location. This operation will move the pointer to the next memory location without impacting the actual value at the memory location. If **ptr** points to a character whose address is 1000, then the above operation will point to the location 1001 because the next character will be available at 1001.

Incrementing a Pointer

We prefer using a pointer in our program instead of an array because the variable pointer can be incremented, unlike the array name which cannot be incremented because it is a constant pointer. The following program increments the variable pointer to access each succeeding element of the array –

```
#include<stdio.h>
const int MAX =3;
int main (){
int var[]={10,100,200};
inti,*ptr;
/* let us have array address in pointer */
ptr=var;
for(i=0;i< MAX;i++)
{
printf("Address of var[%d] = %x\n",i, ptr);
printf("Value of var[%d] = %d\n",i,*ptr);
/* move to the next location */
ptr++;
}
return0;
}
```

OUTPUT:
Address of var[0] = bf882b30
Value of var[0] = 10
Address of var[1] = bf882b34
Value of var[1] = 100
Address of var[2] = bf882b38
Value of var[2] = 200

Decrementing a Pointer

The same considerations apply to decrementing a pointer, which decreases its value by the number of bytes of its data type as shown below –

```
#include<stdio.h>
const int MAX =3;
int main (){
int var[]={10,100,200};
inti,*ptr;
/* let us have array address in pointer */
```

```
ptr=&var[MAX-1];
for(i= MAX;i>0;i—)
{
printf("Address of var[%d] = %x\n",i,ptr);
printf("Value of var[%d] = %d\n",i,*ptr);
/* move to the previous location */
ptr--;
}
return0;
}
```

OUTPUT:

Address of var[3] = bfedbcd8
Value of var[3] = 200
Address of var[2] = bfedbcd4
Value of var[2] = 100
Address of var[1] = bfedbcd0
Value of var[1] = 10

Pointer Comparisons

Pointers may be compared by using relational operators, such as ==, <, and >. If p1 and p2 point to variables that are related to each other, such as elements of the same array, then p1 and p2 can be meaningfully compared.
The following program modifies the previous example – one by incrementing the variable pointer so long as the address to which it points is either less than or equal to the address of the last element of the array, which is &var[MAX - 1] –

```
#include<stdio.h>
const int MAX =3;
Int main (){
int var[]={10,100,200};
inti,*ptr;
/* let us have address of the first element in pointer */
ptr=var;
i=0;
while(ptr<=&var[MAX -1])
{
printf("Address of var[%d] = %x\n",i,ptr);
printf("Value of var[%d] = %d\n",i,*ptr);
/* point to the previous location */
ptr++;
i++;
}
return0;
}
```

OUTPUT:

Address of var[0] = bfdbcb20
Value of var[0] = 10
Address of var[1] = bfdbcb24
Value of var[1] = 100
Address of var[2] = bfdbcb28
Value of var[2] = 200

What is Pointer to Pointer in C?

A pointer to a pointer is a form of multiple indirection, or a chain of pointers. Normally, a pointer contains the address of a variable. When we define a pointer to a pointer, the first pointer contains the address of the second pointer, which points to the location that contains the actual value as shown below.

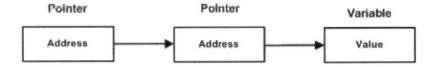

A variable that is a pointer to a pointer must be declared as such. This is done by placing an additional asterisk in front of its name. For example, the following declaration declares a pointer to a pointer of type int –
int **var;
When a target value is indirectly pointed to by a pointer to a pointer, accessing that value requires that the asterisk operator be applied twice, as is shown below in the example –

```
#include<stdio.h>
int main (){
int var;
int*ptr;
int**pptr;
var=3000;
/* take the address of var */
ptr=&var;
/* take the address of ptr using address of operator & */
pptr=&ptr;
/* take the value using pptr */
printf("Value of var = %d\n",var);
printf("Value available at *ptr = %d\n",*ptr);
printf("Value available at **pptr = %d\n",**pptr);
return0;
}
```

OUTPUT:
```
Value of var = 3000
Value available at *ptr = 3000
Value available at **pptr = 3000
```

DIFFERENT WAYS OF PASSING ARGUMENTS

Point	Call by Value	Call by Reference
Copy	Duplicate Copy of Original Parameter is Passed	Actual Copy of Original Parameter is Passed
Modification	No effect on Original Parameter after modifying parameter in function	Original Parameter gets affected if value of parameter changed inside function

Explain pointers to structure in detail

Like we have array of integers, array of pointer etc, we can also have array of structure variables. And to make the use of array of structure variables efficient, we use **pointers of structure type**. We can also have pointer to a single structure variable, but it is mostly used with array of structure variables.

```
structBook
{
 char name[10];
int price;
}
int main()
{
struct Book a;   //Single structure variable
struct Book* ptr;   //Pointer of Structure type
ptr = &a;

struct Book b[10];     //Array of structure variables
struct Book* p;   //Pointer of Structure type
 p = &b;
}
```

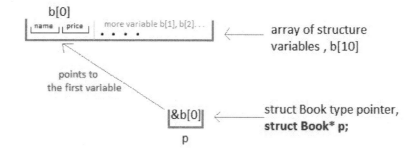

To access members of structure with structure variable, we used the dot . operator. But when we have a pointer of structure type, we use arrow -> to access structure members.

```
struct Book
{
```

```
 char name[10];
int price;
}
int main()
{
struct Book b;
struct Book* ptr = &b;
ptr->name = "Dan Brown";   //Accessing Structure Members
ptr->price = 500;
}
```

Explain pointer to array in detail.

Pointer and Arrays:

When an array is declared, compiler allocates sufficient amount of memory to contain all the elements of the array. Base address which gives location of the first element is also allocated by the compiler.

Suppose we declare an array **arr**,

int arr[5]={ 1, 2, 3, 4, 5 };

Assuming that the base address of **arr** is 1000 and each integer requires two byte, the five element will be stored as follows

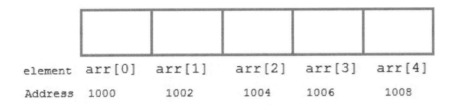

```
element  arr[0]   arr[1]   arr[2]   arr[3]   arr[4]
Address  1000     1002     1004     1006     1008
```

Here variable **arr** will give the base address, which is a constant pointer pointing to the element, **arr[0]**. Therefore **arr** is containing the address of **arr[0]** i.e 1000.
arr *is equal to* **&arr[0]**   // by default

We can declare a pointer of type int to point to the array **arr**.
int *p;
p = arr;
or p = &arr[0]; //both the statements are equivalent.

Now we can access every element of array **arr** using **p++** to move from one element to another.

NOTE : You cannot decrement a pointer once incremented. p-- won't work.

Pointer to Array

As studied above, we can use a pointer to point to an Array, and then we can use that pointer to access the array. Lets have an example,

```
inti;
inta[5] = {1, 2, 3, 4, 5};
int *p = a;  // same as int*p = &a[0]
for (i=0; i<5; i++)
{
printf("%d", *p);
 p++;
}
```

In the above program, the pointer ***p** will print all the values stored in the array one by one. We can also use the Base address (**a** in above case) to act as pointer and print all the values.

Replacing the **printf("%d", *p);** statement of above example, with below mentioned statements. Lets see what will be the result.

printf("%d", a[i]); ⟶ prints the array, by incrementing index

printf("%d", i[a]); ⟶ this will also print elements of array

printf("%d", a+i); ⟶ This will print address of all the array elements

printf("%d", *(a+i)); ⟶ Will print value of array element.

printf("%d", *a); ⟶ will print value of a[0] only

a++; ⟶ Compile time error, we cannot change base address of the array.

Pointer to Multidimensional Array

A multidimensional array is of form, a[i][j]. Lets see how we can make a pointer point to such an array. As we know now, name of the array gives its base address. In a[i][j], a will give the base address of this array, even a+0+0 will also give the base address, that is the address of **a[0][0]** element.

Here is the generalised form for using pointer with multidimensional arrays.

((ptr + i) + j) *is same as* **a[i][j]**

Pointer and Character strings

Pointer can also be used to create strings. Pointer variables of **char** type are treated as string.

char *str = "Hello";

This creates a string and stores its address in the pointer variable **str**. The pointer **str** now points to the first character of the string "Hello". Another important thing to note that string created using **char** pointer can be assigned a value at **runtime**.

```
char *str;
str = "hello";   //this is Legal
```
The content of the string can be printed using printf() and puts().
```
printf("%s", str);
puts(str);
```

Notice that **str** is pointer to the string, it is also name of the string. Therefore we do not need to use indirection operator *.

Array of Pointers

We can also have array of pointers. Pointers are very helpful in handling character array with rows of varying length.
```
char *name[3]={
          "Adam",
          "chris",
          "Deniel"
     };
```
                    //Now see same array without using pointer
```
char name[3][20]= {
          "Adam",
          "chris",
          "Deniel"
        };
```

Using Pointer

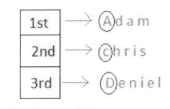

char* name[3]

Only 3 locations for pointers, which will point to the first character of their respective strings.

Without Pointer

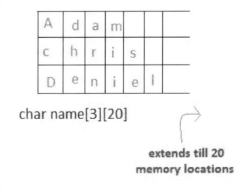

char name[3][20]

extends till 20 memory locations

In the second approach memory wastage is more, hence it is preferred to use pointer in such cases.

Give an introduction to shell programming.

An Operating is made of many components but its two prime components are -
* Kernel
* Shell

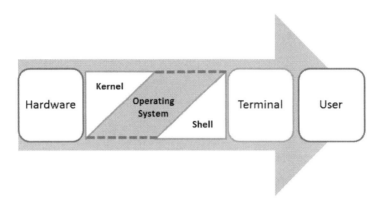

Kernel is at the nucleus of a computer. It makes the communication between the hardware and software possible. While the Kernel is the innermost part of an operating system, a shell is the outermost one.

A **shell** in a Linux operating system takes input from you in the form of commands, processes it, and then gives an output. It is the interface through which a user works on the programs, commands and scripts. A shell is accessed by a terminal which runs it.

When you run the terminal, the Shell issues **a command prompt (usually $),** where you can type your input, which is then executed when you hit the Enter key. The output or the result is thereafter displayed on the terminal.

The Shell wraps around the delicate interior of an Operating system protecting it from accidental damage. Hence the name **Shell**.

Types of Shell

There are two main shells in Linux:

1. The **Bourne Shell**: The prompt for this shell is $ and its derivatives are listed below:

* POSIX shell also known as sh
* Korn Shell also known as sh
* **Bourne Again SH**ell also known as bash (most popular)

2. **The C shell**: The prompt for this shell is % and its subcategories are:

* C shell also known as csh
* Tops C shell also known as tcsh

What is Shell scripting and why do I need it?

Writing a series of command for the shell to execute is called shell scripting. It can combine lengthy and repetitive sequences of commands into a single and simple script, which can be stored and executed anytime. This reduces the effort required by the end user.

SUMMARY:

- Kernel is the nucleus of the operating systems and it communicates between hardware and software
- Shell is a program which interprets user commands through CLI like Terminal
- The Bourne shell and the C shell are the most used shells in Linux
- Shell scripting is writing a series of command for the shell to execute
- Shell variables store the value of a string or a number for the shell to read
- Shell scripting can help you create complex programs containing conditional statements, loops and functions

What is C shell?

C shell is a Unix shell created in 1979 by Bill Joy soon after the Bourne shell was released in 1977. Although the latter went on to be the standard shell for Unix, C shell is still popular in BSD distributions. C shell's scripting syntax is modelled after the C language in some aspects. Small programs can be created by writing scripts using the C shell syntax.
The Bourne shell is also an option to create Unix scripts but if you are reading this book you probably decided the C shell fits your requirements better. Deciding to use a Unix script at all means that the requirements of the program are rather simple, such as automating the usage of either standard or custom Unix tools. Complex logic or speed sensitive functions should be written in a more appropriate language as custom tools.

PROGRAMS

PROGRAM 1

Q: WRITE A PROGRAM TO PRINT "HELLO WORLD" ON YOUR SCREEN.

A:

```c
#include <stdio.h>

int main()
{
    printf("Hello World\n");

    return 0;
}
```

OUTPUT:

```
Hello World
Program ended with exit code: 0
```

PROGRAM 2

Q: WRITE A PROGRAM TO ADD TWO NUMBERS ON YOUR SCREEN.

A:

```c
#include<stdio.h>

int main()
{
    int a , b ;
    a=10;
    b=20;
    printf( "The sum of two numbers is : %d\n",a+b);

    return 0;
}
```

OUTPUT:

```
The sum of two numbers is : 30
Program ended with exit code: 0
```

PROGRAM 3

Q: WRITE A PROGRAM TO SWAP TO NUMBERS USING A TEMPORARY VARIABLE.

A:
```c
#include<stdio.h>
int main ()
{
  int a, b, temp;        //declaration of three variables
  a = 10;
  b = 20;
  printf ("Values before swapping a=%d , b=%d \n", a, b);
  temp = a;              // assigning value of a to temp
  a = b;                 // assigning value of b to a
  b = temp;              // assigning value of temp to b
  printf ("Values after swapping are a=%d , b=%d \n ", a, b);

  return 0;
}
```

OUTPUT:

```
Values before swapping a=10 , b=20
Values after swapping are a=20 , b=10
```

PROGRAM 4

Q: WRITE A PROGRAM TO SWAP TWO NUMBERS WITHOUT USING TEMPORARY VARIABLE.

A:
```c
#include<stdio.h>
int main()
{
    int a=10;
    int b=20;
    printf("Values before swapping a=%d , b=%d \n",a ,b);
    a=a+b;
    b=a-b;
    a=a-b;
    printf("Values after swapping are a=%d , b=%d \n",a ,b);

    return 0;
}
```

OUTPUT:

```
Values before swapping a=10 , b=20
Values after swapping are a=20 , b=10
```

PROGRAM 5

Q: WRITE A PROGRAM TO SHOW VARIOUS ARITHMETIC OPERATIONS.

A:
```c
#include<stdio.h>
int main ()
{
  int a = 10;
  int b = 20;
  printf ("sum of a and b is : %d\n", a + b);
  printf ("difference between a and b is : %d\n", b - a);
  printf ("product of a and b is : %d\n", a * b);
  printf ("b divided by a is : %d\n", b / a);
  printf ("remainder when b is divided by a is :%d\n", b % a);

  return 0;
}
```

OUTPUT:

```
sum of a and b is : 30
difference between a and b is : 10
product of a and b is : 200
b divided by a is : 2
remainder when b is divided by a is :0
```

PROGRAM 6

Q: WRITE A PROGRAM TO FIND SIMPLE INTEREST.

A:
```c
#include<stdio.h>
int main ()
{
  float p, r, t, si;
  printf ("Enter principle, rate of interest and time : \n");
  scanf ("%f \n %f \n %f", &p, &r, &t);
  si = (p * r * t) / 100;
  printf ("Simple interest is :%f", si);

  return 0;
}
```

OUTPUT:

```
Enter principle, rate of interest and time :
1200
2
3
Simple interest is :72.000000
```

PROGRAM 7

Q: WRITE A PROGRAM TO FIND GREATEST OF THREE NUMBERS.

A:
```c
#include<stdio.h>
int main ()
{
  int a = 10;
  int b = 20;
  int c = 15;
  if (a > b)
   {
     if (a > c)
       printf ("%d is greatest \n", a);
     else
       printf ("%d is greatest \n", c);
   }
  else
   {
     if (b > c)
       printf ("%d is greatest \n", b);
     else
       printf ("%d is greatest \n", c);
   }

  return 0;
}
```

OUTPUT:

```
20 is greatest
Program ended with exit code: 0
```

PROGRAM 8

Q: WRITE A PROGRAM TO FIND GREATEST OF TWO NUMBERS USING CONDITIONAL OPERATOR.

A:

```c
#include<stdio.h>

int main ()
{

  int a = 10, b = 15, big;

  big = (a > b ? a : b);

  printf ("%d is greatest\n", big);

  return 0;

}
```

OUTPUT:

```
15 is greatest
Program ended with exit code: 0
```

PROGRAM 9

Q: WRITE A PROGRAM FIND WHETHER THE NUMBER IS ODD OR EVEN.

A:
```c
#include<stdio.h>

int main ()
{
  int a;
  printf ("Enter a number of your choice\n");
  scanf ("%d", &a);
  if (a % 2 == 0)
    printf ("number is even\n");
  else
    printf ("number is odd\n");

  return 0;

}
```

OUTPUT:

```
Enter a number of your choice
327
number is odd
Program ended with exit code: 0
```

PROGRAM 10

Q: WRITE A PROGRAM TO CHECK WHETHER THE YEAR IS LEAP YEAR OR NOT.

A:
```c
#include<stdio.h>
int main()
{
    int year;
    printf("enter the year: ");
    scanf("%d", &year) ;
    if( year%4==0 && year%100!=0 || year%400==0)
    {
        printf("%d is leap year\n ", year);
    }
    else
        printf("%d is not a leap year\n ",year );

    return 0;
}
```

OUTPUT:

```
enter the year: 1800
1800 is not a leap year
Program ended with exit code: 0
```

PROGRAM 11

Q: WRITE A PROGRAM TO FIND SUM OF DIGITS OF A NUMBER.

A:
```c
#include<stdio.h>
int main ()
{
  int a, num, sum = 0;
  printf ("enter a number of your choice \n");
  scanf ("%d", &num);        //example 125
  while (num != 0)
   {
     a = num % 10;           //5    //2  //1
     sum = sum + a;          //5    //7  //8
     num = num / 10;         //12   //1  //0(loop terminated)
   }
  printf ("The sum of digits of a number is : %d\n", sum);

  return 0;

}
```

OUTPUT:

```
enter a number of your choice
125
The sum of digits of a number is : 8
Program ended with exit code: 0
```

PROGRAM 12

Q: WRITE A PROGRAM TO FIND FACTORIAL OF A NUMBER.

A:
```c
#include<stdio.h>
int main ()
{
  int i, num, fact = 1;
  printf ("Enter the number of your choice \n");
  scanf ("%d", &num);
  for (i = 1; i <= num; i++)
   {
     fact = fact * i;
   }
  printf ("factorial of number is : %d\n", fact);

  return 0;

}
```

OUTPUT:

```
Enter the number of your choice
5
factorial of number is : 120
Program ended with exit code: 0
```

PROGRAM 13

Q: WRITE A PROGRAM TO FIND PERFECT DIVISORS OF A NUMBER.

A:
```c
#include<stdio.h>
int main ()
{
  int i, num;
  printf ("Enter the number of your choice : \n");
  scanf ("%d", &num);
  printf ("The divisors of a number are :- \n");
  for (i = 1; i <= num; i++)
    {
      if (num % i == 0)
        printf ("%d\n", i);
    }

  return 0;
}
```

OUTPUT:

```
Enter the number of your choice :
24
The divisors of a number are :-
1
2
3
4
6
8
12
24
Program ended with exit code: 0
```

PROGRAM 14

Q: WRITE A PROGRAM TO FIND WHETHER THE NUMBER IS PRIME OR NOT.

A:
```c
#include<stdio.h>
int main ()
{
  int i, num, a = 0;
  printf ("Enter a number \n");
  scanf ("%d", &num);
  for (i = 2; i <= num / 2; i++)
   {
     if (num % i == 0)
       a = 1;
     break;
   }
  if (a == 0)
   {
     printf ("number is a prime\n");
   }
  else
    printf ("number is not a prime\n");
  return 0;
}
```

OUTPUT:

```
Enter a number
19
number is a prime
Program ended with exit code: 0
```

PROGRAM 15

Q: WRITE A PROGRAM TO GENERATE SERIES OF PRIME NUMBERS.
A:

```c
#include<stdio.h>
int main ()
{
  int i, j, num, flag;
  printf ("enter the number of till you want prime numbers : ");
  scanf ("%d", &num);
  printf ("the prime numbers are : \n");
  for (i = 1; i <= num; i++)
    {
      flag = 0;
      for (j = 1; j <= i; j++)
        {
          if (i % j == 0)
            flag++;
        }
      if (flag == 2)
        printf ("%d\n", i);
    }
  return 0;
}
```

OUTPUT:

```
enter the number of till you want prime numbers : 37
the prime numbers are :
2
3
5
7
11
13
17
19
23
29
31
37
Program ended with exit code: 0
```

PROGRAM 16

Q: WRITE A PROGRAM TO GENERATE FIBONACCI SERIES.
A:

```c
#include<stdio.h>
int main ()
{
  int i, x = 0, y = 1, b, n;
  printf ("Enter the number of terms :");
  scanf ("%d", &n);
  printf ("%d\n%d\n", x, y);
  for (i = 2; i <= n; i++)
   {
     b = x + y;
     printf ("%d\n", b);
     x = y;
     y = b;
   }
  return 0;
}
```

OUTPUT:-

```
Enter the number of terms :7
0
1
1
2
3
5
8
13
Program ended with exit code: 0
```

PROGRAM 17

Q:WRITE A PROGRAM TO CHECK WHETHER THE NUMBER IS PALINDROME OR NOT.

A:

```c
#include<stdio.h>
int main ()
{
  int rem, rev = 0, num, temp;
  printf ("Enter a number of your choice : ");
  scanf ("%d", &num);
  temp = num;
  while (num != 0)
   {
     rem = num % 10;
     rev = rev * 10 + rem;
     num = num / 10;
   }
  printf ("The reverse of number is :%d \n", rev);
  if (rev == temp)
    printf ("The number is palindrome\n");
  else
    printf ("The number is not a palindrome\n");

  return 0;
}
```

OUTPUT:

```
Enter a number of your choice : 12121
The reverse of number is :12121
The number is palindrome
Program ended with exit code: 0
```

PROGRAM 18

Q: WRITE A PROGRAM TO FIND HCF AND LCM OF A NUMBER.
A:

```c
#include<stdio.h>
int main ()
{
  int a, b, x, y, i, temp, hcf, lcm;
  printf ("enter first number: ");
  scanf ("%d", &x);
  printf ("\nenter second number: ");
  scanf ("%d", &y);
  a = x;
  b = y;
  while (b != 0)
   {
     temp = b;
     b = a % b;
     a = temp;
   }
  hcf = a;
  printf ("The hcf of numbers is : %d", hcf);
  printf ("\nThe lcm of numbers is :%d\n", x * y / hcf);
  return 0;
}
```

OUTPUT:

```
enter first number: 15
enter second number: 25
The hcf of numbers is : 5
The lcm of numbers is :75
Program ended with exit code: 0
```

PROGRAM 19

Q: WRITE A PROGRAM TO FIND ANSWER FOR BASE TO THE POWER.
A:
```c
#include<stdio.h>
int main ()
{
  int base, power, i, a = 1;
  printf ("Enter the base:");
  scanf ("%d", &base);
  printf ("Enter the power:");
  scanf ("%d", &power);
  for (i = 1; i <= power; i++)
   {
     a = base * a;
   }
  printf ("Answer is : %d\n", a);

  return 0;
}
```

OUTPUT:

```
Enter the base: 5
Enter the power: 3
Answer is : 125
Program ended with exit code: 0
```

PROGRAM 20

Q: WRITE A PROGRAM TO FIND THE NUMBER OF TIMES THE DIGIT HAS OCCURRED IN A NUMBER.

A:

```c
#include<stdio.h>
int main ()
{
  int r, num, count = 0, n;
  printf ("Enter the number : ");
  scanf ("%d", &num);
  printf ("Enter the digit : ");
  scanf ("%d", &n);
  while (num != 0)
   {
     r = num % 10;
     if (r == n)
       {
          count++;
       }
     num = num / 10;
   }
  printf ("The occurrence is : %d times\n", count);

return 0;
}
```

OUTPUT:

```
Enter the number : 3222434
Enter the digit : 2
The occurrence is : 3 times
Program ended with exit code: 0
```

PROGRAM 21

Q: WRITE A PROGRAM TO GENERATE TABLE OF A NUMBER.
A:
```c
#include<stdio.h>
int main ()
{
  int n, i, a;
  printf ("Enter a number : ");
  scanf ("%d", &n);
  for (i = 1; i <= 10; i++)
   {
     a = n * i;
     printf ("%d X %d = %d \n", n, i, a);
   }

  return 0;
}
```

OUTPUT:

```
Enter a number : 5
5 X 1 = 5
5 X 2 = 10
5 X 3 = 15
5 X 4 = 20
5 X 5 = 25
5 X 6 = 30
5 X 7 = 35
5 X 8 = 40
5 X 9 = 45
5 X 10 = 50
Program ended with exit code: 0
```

PROGRAM 22

Q: WRITE A PROGRAM TO CHECK WHETHER THE NUMBER IS AMSTRONG NUMBER OR NOT.

A:
```c
#include<stdio.h>
int main ()
{
  int res = 0, rem, num, temp;
  printf ("Enter a number of your choice : ");
  scanf ("%d", &num);
  temp = num;
  while (num != 0)
   {
     rem = num % 10;
     res = res + rem * rem * rem;
     num = num / 10;
   }
  printf ("The result is : %d \n", res);
  if (res == temp)
    printf ("The number is amstrong");
  else
    printf ("the number is not amstrong");

  return 0;
}
```

OUTPUT:

```
Enter a number of your choice : 153
The result is : 153
The number is amstrong
Program ended with exit code: 0
```

PROGRAM 23

Q: WRITE A PROGRAM TO CHECK WHETHER THE NUMBER IS STRONG OR NOT.

A:
```c
#include<stdio.h>
int main ()
{
  int rem, sum = 0, f = 1, num, temp, j;
  printf ("Enter the number : ");
  scanf ("%d", &num);
  temp = num;
  while (num != 0)
   {
     f = 1;
     rem = num % 10;
     for (j = 1; j <= rem; j++)
       {
         f = f * j;
       }
     sum = sum + f;
     num = num / 10;
   }
  printf ("The sum is : %d \n", sum);
  if (sum == temp)
    printf ("The number is strong\n");
  else
    printf ("Not strong\n");
}
```

OUTPUT:

```
Enter the number : 145
The sum is : 145
The number is strong
Program ended with exit code: 0
```

PROGRAM 24

Q: WRITE A PROGRAM TO PRINT THE SUM OF ODD SERIES.

A:
```c
#include<stdio.h>
int
main ()
{
  int sum = 0, n, i;
  printf ("enter the number of terms :");
  scanf ("%d", &n);
  for (i = 1; i <= n*2; i += 2)
   {
     sum = sum + i;
   }
  printf ("sum is : %d\n", sum);

  return 0;

}
```

OUTPUT:

```
enter the number of terms :5
sum is : 25
Program ended with exit code: 0
```

Q: WRITE A PROGRAM TO PRINT THE SUM OF EVEN SERIES.

A:
```c
#include<stdio.h>
int
main ()
{
  int sum = 0, n, i;
  printf ("enter the number of terms :");
  scanf ("%d", &n);
  for (i – 2; i <– n*2; i +– 2)
   {
     sum = sum + i;
   }
  printf ("sum is : %d\n", sum);

  return 0;

}
```

OUTPUT:

```
enter the number of terms :5
sum is : 30
Program ended with exit code: 0
```

PROGRAM 26

Q: WRITE A PROGRAM FIND COMPOUND INTEREST.

A:
```c
#include<stdio.h>
#include<math.h>
int main ()
{
  float p, r, i, t, ci, a, amount = 1;
  printf ("Type the principle : ");
  scanf ("%f", &p);
  printf ("Type the interest rate : ");
  scanf ("%f", &r);
  printf ("Type the period in years: ");
  scanf ("%f", &t);
  i = 1 + (r / 100);
  for (a = 1; a <= t; a++)
   {
     amount = amount * i;
   }
  amount = amount * p;
  ci = amount - p;
  //or use ci=p*pow(i,t)-p; directly
  printf ("Your compound interest is : %.2f\n", ci);
  return 0;
}
```

OUTPUT:

```
Type the principle : 1200
Type the interest rate : 2
Type the period in years: 3
Your compound interest is : 73.45
Program ended with exit code: 0
```

PROGRAM 27

Q: WRITE A PROGRAM TO GENERATE A PASCAL TRIANGLE(for 5 rows).

A:
```c
#include<stdio.h>
#include<math.h>
int main ()
{
    int a, i, n;
    printf("pascal's triangle for 5 rows:\n");
        printf ("1\n");
        for (i    1; i < 5; i++)
        {
            a = pow (11, i);
            printf ("%d\n", a);
        }
        return 0;
}
```

OUTPUT:

```
pascal's triangle for 5 rows:
1
11
121
1331
14641
Program ended with exit code: 0
```

PROGRAM 28

Q: WRITE A PROGRAM TO FIND SUM OF SERIES (1*1)+(2*2)+(3*3)..(N*N)

A:
```c
#include<stdio.h>
int main ()
{
  int i, n, sum = 0;
  n = 10;
  for (i = 1; i <= n; i++)
   {
     sum = sum + i * i;
   }
  printf ("Sum: %d\n", sum);

  return 0;

}
```

OUTPUT:

```
Sum: 385
Program ended with exit code: 0
```

PROGRAM 29

Q:WRITE A PROGRAM TO FIND SUM OF SERIES 1! + 2! + 3! .. N!.

A:
```c
#include<stdio.h>
int main ()

{ long fact(int n);
  int i ,sum=0,n;
  n=5;
  for(i=1;i<=n;i++)
  {
     sum=sum+fact(i);
  }
  printf("SUM IS : %d\n",sum);
}
long fact(int n)
{
   int f=1,i;
   for(i=1;i<=n;i++)
   {
      f=f*i;
   }
   return f;
}
```

OUTPUT:

```
SUM IS : 153
Program ended with exit code: 0
```

PROGRAM 30

Q: WRITE A PROGRAM TO FIND SUM OF SERIES(1^1)+(2^2)+(3^3)..(N^N)

A:
```c
#include<stdio.h>
#include<math.h>
int main()
{
    int i,sum=0,n;
    printf("Enter number of terms: ");
    scanf("%d",&n);
    for(i=1;i<=n;i++)
    {
        sum=sum+pow(i,i);
    }
    printf("Sum is : %d\n",sum);
    return 0;

}
```

OUTPUT:

```
Enter number of terms: 5
Sum is : 3413
Program ended with exit code: 0
```

PROGRAM 31

Q: WRITE A PROGRAM TO FIND SUM OF SERIES [(1^1)/1!] + [(2^2)/2!] + [(3^3)/3!]....[(N^N)/N!].

A:
```c
#include<stdio.h>
#include<math.h>
long fact(int);
int main ()
{

  int i, n;
  double sum = 0.0;
  printf ("Enter number of terms: ");
  scanf ("%d", &n);
  for (i = 1; i <= n; i++)
   {
     sum = sum + (pow (i, i)) / fact (i);
   }
  printf ("sum is : %lf\n", sum);
}

long fact(int n)
{
  int f = 1, i;
  for (i = 1; i <= n; i++)
   {
     f = f * i;
   }
  return f;
}
```

OUTPUT:

```
Enter number of terms: 8
sum is : 688.511310
Program ended with exit code: 0
```

PROGRAM 32

Q: WRITE A PROGRAM FIND THE SUM OF SERIES 1/2 - 2/3 + 3/4 - 4/5 + 5/6 - ...... n

A:
```c
#include<stdio.h>
int main ()
{
  double i, n, sum = 0;
  n = 12;
  for (i = 1; i <= n; i++)
   {
     if ((int) i % 2 == 1)
      sum = sum + i / (i + 1);
     else
      sum = sum - i / (i + 1);
   }
  printf ("Sum: %lf\n", sum);
  return 0;
}
```

OUTPUT:

```
Sum: -0.269866
Program ended with exit code: 0
```

PROGRAM 33

Q: WRITE A PROGRAM TO GENERATE SERIES 1 2 3 6 9 18 27 54…

A:
```c
#include <stdio.h>
int main ()
{
  int q= 1, p = 2, n, i;
  printf ("Enter number of terms : ");
  scanf ("%d",&n);
  printf ("%d\n%d\n", q, p);
  for (i = 3; i <= n; i++)
   {
     if (i % 2 == 1)
       {
         q = q * 3;
         printf ("%d\n", q);
       }
     if (i % 2 == 0)
       {
         p = p * 3;
         printf ("%d\n", p);
       }
   }
  return 0;
}
```

OUTPUT:

```
Enter number of terms : 8
1
2
3
6
9
18
27
54
Program ended with exit code: 0
```

95

PROGRAM 34

Q: WRITE A PROGRAM TO GENERATE SERIES 2 15 41 80 132 197 275 366 470 587

A:
```c
#include <stdio.h>
int main ()
{
  int add = 2, i, n;
  printf ("Enter the number of terms: ");
  scanf ("%d", &n);
  for (i = 0; i < n; i++)
   {
     add = add + 13 * i;
     printf ("%d\n", add);
   }
     return 0;
}
```

OUTPUT:

```
Enter the number of terms: 10
2
15
41
80
132
197
275
366
470
587
Program ended with exit code: 0
```

Q: WRITE A PROGRAM TO GENERATE A SERIES 1 3 8 15 27 50 92 169 311 572..

A:

```c
#include<stdio.h>
int main()
{
    int p=1, q=3, r=4,n, sum, i;
    printf("Enter terms: ");
    scanf("%d",&n);
    printf("%d\n%d\n",p,q);
    for(i=2; i<n; i++)
    {
        sum = p+q+r;
        printf("%d\n",sum);
      p = q;
      q = r;
      r = sum;
    }
}
```

OUTPUT:

```
Enter terms: 5
1
3
8
15
27
Program ended with exit code: 0
```

PROGRAM 36

Q: WRITE A PROGRAM TO PRINT STAR PATTERN 1(RIGHT ANGLE TRIANGLE).

A:
```c
#include<stdio.h>

int main()
{
    int i,j;
    for(i=5;i>=1;i--)
    {
        for(j=1;j<=i;j++)
        {
            printf("*");
        }
        printf("\n");
    }
    return 0;
}
```

OUTPUT:

```
*****
****
***
**
*
Program ended with exit code: 0
```

PROGRAM 37:

Q: WRITE A PROGRAM TO PRINT STAR PATTERN 2 (RIGHT ANGLE TRIANGLE).

A:
```c
#include<stdio.h>

int main()
{
    int i,j;
    for(i=1;i<=5;i++)
    {
        for(j=1;j<=i;j++)
        {
            printf("*");
        }
        printf("\n");
    }
    return 0;
}
```

OUTPUT:

```
*
**
***
****
*****
Program ended with exit code: 0
```

99

PROGRAM 38

Q: WRITE A PROGRAM TO PRINT STAR PATTERN 3 (RIGHT ANGLE TRIANGLE)

A:
```c
#include<stdio.h>
int main()
{
    int i,j,k;
    for(i=1;i<=5;i++)
    {
        for(j=1;j<i;j++)
        {
            printf(" ");
        }
        for(k=5;k>=i;k--)
        {
            printf("*");
        }
        printf("\n");
    }
    return 0;
}
```

OUTPUT:

```
*****
 ****
  ***
   **
    *
Program ended with exit code: 0
```

PROGRAM 39

Q: WRITE A PROGRAM TO PRINT STAR PATTERN 4 (RIGHT ANGLE TRIANGLE).

A:
```c
#include<stdio.h>
int main()
{
    int i,j,k;
    for(i=5;i>=1;i--)
    {
        for(j=1;j<i;j++)
        {
            printf(" ");
        }
        for(k=5;k>=i;k--)
        {
            printf("*");
        }
        printf("\n");
    }
    return 0;
}
```

OUTPUT:

```
    *
   **
  ***
 ****
*****
Program ended with exit code: 0
```

PROGRAM 40

Q: WRITE A PROGRAM TO PRINT STAR PATTERN 5 (UPRIGHT TRIANGLE)

A:
```c
#include<stdio.h>
int main()
{
    int i,j,k;
    for(i=1;i<=5;i++)
    {
        for(j=i;j<5;j++)
        {
            printf(" ");
        }
        for(k=1;k<=i*2-1;k++)
        {
            printf("*");
        }
        printf("\n");
    }
    return 0;
}
```

OUTPUT:

```
    *
   ***
  *****
 *******
*********
Program ended with exit code: 0
```

102

PROGRAM 41

Q:WRITE A PROGRAM TO PRINT STAR PATTERN 6 (INVERTED TRIANGLE)

A:
```c
#include<stdio.h>
int main()
{
    int i,j,k;
    for(i=5;i>=1;i--)
    {
        for(j=5;j>i;j--)
        {
            printf(" ");
        }
        for(k=1;k<=i*2-1;k++)
        {
            printf("*");
        }
        printf("\n");
    }
    return 0;
}
```

OUTPUT:

```
*********
 *******
  *****
   ***
    *
Program ended with exit code: 0
```

103

PROGRAM 42

Q: WRITE A PROGRAM TO PRINT STAR PATTERN 7 (DIAMOND).
A:

```c
#include<stdio.h>
int main()
{   int i, j, k;
    for(i=1; i<=5; i++)
    {   for(j=i ;j<5; j++)
        {
            printf(" ");
        }
        for(k=1; k<=i*2-1; k++)
        {
            printf("*");
        }
        printf("\n");
    }
    for(i=4; i>=1; i--)
    {   for(j=5; j>i; j--)
        {
            printf(" ");
        }
        for(k=1; k<=i*2-1; k++)
        {
            printf("*");
        }
        printf("\n");
    } return 0;
}
```

OUTPUT:

```
        *
       ***
      *****
     *******
    *********
     *******
      *****
       ***
        *
Program ended with exit code: 0
```

104

PROGRAM 43

Q: WRITE A PROGRAM TO PRINT NUMBER PATTERN 1 (RIGTH ANGLE TRIANGLE).

A:
```c
#include<stdio.h>
int main()
{
    int i,j;
    for(i=5;i>=1;i--)
    {
        for(j=1;j<=i;j++)
        {
            printf("%d",j);
        }
        printf("\n");
    }
    return 0;
}
```

OUTPUT:

```
12345
1234
123
12
1
Program ended with exit code: 0
```

PROGRAM 44

Q: WRITE A PROGRAM TO PRINT NUMBER PATTERN 2 (RIGHT ANGLE TRIANGLE).

A:
```c
#include<stdio.h>
int main()
{
    int i,j;
    for(i=1;i<=5;i++)
    {
        for(j=1;j<=i;j++)
        {
            printf("%d",i);
        }
        printf("\n");
    }
    return 0;
}
```

OUTPUT:

```
1
22
333
4444
55555
Program ended with exit code: 0
```

PROGRAM 45

Q: WRITE A PROGRAM TO PRINT NUMBER PATTERN 3 (RIGHT ANGLE TRIANGLE).

A:
```c
#include<stdio.h>
int main()
{
    int i,j,k;
    for(i=1;i<=5;i++)
    {
        for(j=1;j<i;j++)
        {
            printf(" ");
        }
        for(k=5;k>=i;k--)
        {
            printf("%d",k);
        }
        printf("\n");
    }
    return 0;
}
```

OUTPUT:

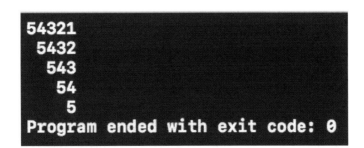

107

PROGRAM 46

Q: WRITE A PROGRAM TO PRINT NUMBER PATTERN 4(RIGHT ANGLE TRIANGLE).

A:
```c
#include<stdio.h>
int main()
{
    int i,j,k;
    for(i=5;i>=1;i--)
    {
        for(j=1;j<i;j++)
        {
            printf(" ");
        }
        for(k=5;k>=i;k--)
        {
            printf("%d",j);
        }
        printf("\n");
    }
    return 0;
}
```

OUTPUT:

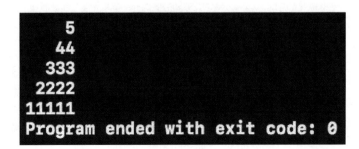

108

PROGRAM 47

Q: WRITE A PROGRAM TO PRINT NUMBER PATTERN 5 (UPRIGHT TRIANGLE) .

A:
```c
#include<stdio.h>
int main()
{
    int i,j,k,n=1;
    for(i=1;i<=4;i++)
    {
        for(j=i;j<=4;j++)
        {
            printf(" ");
        }
        for(k=1;k<=i;k++)
        {
            printf("%d ",n++);
        }
        printf("\n");
    }
    return 0;
}
```

OUTPUT:

```
     1
    2 3
   4 5 6
  7 8 9 10
Program ended with exit code: 0
```

PROGRAM 48

Q: WRITE A PROGRAM TO PRINT NUMBER PATTERN 6 (INVERTED TRIANGLE) .

A:
```c
#include<stdio.h>
int main()
{
    int i,j,k,n=10;
    for(i=4;i>=1;i--)
    {
        for(j=4;j>i;j--)
        {
            printf(" ");
        }
        for(k=1;k<=i;k++)
        {
            printf("%d ",n--);
        }
        printf("\n");
    }
    return 0;
}
```

OUTPUT:

```
10 9 8 7
  6 5 4
   3 2
    1
Program ended with exit code: 0
```

PROGRAM 49

Q: WRITE A PROGRAM TO PRINT NUMBER PATTERN 7 (UPRIGHT TRIANGLE) .

A:
```c
#include<stdio.h>
int main()
{
    int i,j,k;
    for(i=1;i<=5;i++)
    {
        for(j=i;j<5;j++)
        {
            printf(" ");
        }
        for(k=1;k<=i;k++)
        {
            printf("%d ",i);
        }
        printf("\n");
    }
    return 0;
}
```

OUTPUT:

```
    1
   2 2
  3 3 3
 4 4 4 4
5 5 5 5 5
Program ended with exit code: 0
```

111

PROGRAM 50

Q: WRITE A PROGRAM TO PRINT NUMBER PATTERN 8 (DIAMOND).

A:
```c
#include<stdio.h>
int main()
{
    int i,j,k;
    for(i=1;i<=5;i++)
    {
        for(j=i;j<5;j++)
        {
            printf(" ");
        }
        for(k=1;k<=i;k++)
        {
            printf("%d ",i);
        }
        printf("\n");
    }
    for(i=4;i>=1;i--)
    {
        for(j=4;j>=i;j--)
        {
            printf(" ");
        }
        for(k=1;k<=i;k++)
        {
            printf("%d ",i);
        }
        printf("\n");
    }
    return 0;
}
```

OUTPUT:

```
    1
   2 2
  3 3 3
 4 4 4 4
5 5 5 5 5
 4 4 4 4
  3 3 3
   2 2
    1
Program ended with exit code: 0
```

PROGRAM 51

Q: WRITE A PROGRAM TO PRINT THE SPECIAL PATTERN GIVEN BELOW.

A:
```c
#include<stdio.h>
int main()
{
    int i, j;
    for(i=1;i<=5;i++)
    {
        for(j=1;j<=5;j++)
        {
            if(i==1|| i==5|| j==5|| j==1)
                printf("5");
            else
                printf("*");
        }
        printf("\n");

    }
    return 0;
}
```

OUTPUT:

```
55555
5***5
5***5
5***5
55555
Program ended with exit code: 0
```

PROGRAM 52

Q: WRITE A PROGRAM TO PRINT THE SPECIAL PATTERN GIVEN BELOW.

A:

```c
#include<stdio.h>
int main()
{
    int i, j;
    for(i=5;i>=1;i--)
    {
        for(j=1;j<=5;j++)
        {
            if(j<=i)
                printf("%d",j);
            else
                printf("*");
        }
        for(j=5;j>=1;j--)
        {
            if(j<=i)
                printf("%d",j);
            else
                printf("*");
        }
        printf("\n");

    }

    return 0;

}
```

OUTPUT:

```
1234554321
1234**4321
123****321
12******21
1********1
Program ended with exit code: 0
```

PROGRAM 53

Q: WRITE A PROGRAM TO PRINT THE SPECIAL PATTERN GIVEN BELOW.

A:

```c
#include<stdio.h>
int main()
{
    int i ,j;
    for(i=1;i<=5;i++)
    {
        for(j=1;j<=5;j++)
        {
            if(j<=i)
                printf("%d",j);
            else
                printf(" ");
        }
        for(j=5;j>=1;j--)
        {
            if(j<=i)
                printf("%d",j);
            else
                printf(" ");
        }
        printf("\n");
    }

    return 0;

}
```

OUTPUT:

```
1         1
12        21
123     321
1234   4321
1234554321
Program ended with exit code: 0
```

PROGRAM 54

Q: WRITE A PROGRAM TO FIND THE FACTORIAL USING A FUNCTION.

A:
```c
#include<stdio.h>
int fact(int);
int main()
{
    int n , result;

    printf("Enter the number : ");
    scanf("%d",&n);

    result=fact(n);

    printf("The factorial of a number is : %d\n",result);
    return 0;
}

int fact(int n)
{
    int i, fac=1;
    for(i=1;i<=n;i++)
    {
        fac=fac*i;
    }
    return(fac);
}
```

OUTPUT:

```
Enter the number : 5
The factorial of a number is : 120
Program ended with exit code: 0
```

PROGRAM 55

Q: WRITE A PROGRAM TO FIND GREATEST COMMON DIVISOR OF THE TWO NUMBERS.

A:
```c
#include<stdio.h>
int gcd(int, int);

int main()
{
    int x, y, result;

    printf("Enter the number : ");
    scanf("%d",&x);
    printf("Enter the second number: ");
    scanf("%d",&y);

    result=gcd(x, y);

    printf("The GCD of numbers is : %d\n",result);
    return 0;
}

int gcd(int a, int b)
{
    while(a!=b)
    {
        if(a>b)
            a=a-b;
        else
            b=b-a;
    }
    return(a);
}
```

OUTPUT:

```
Enter the number : 10
Enter the second number: 15
The GCD of numbers is : 5
Program ended with exit code: 0
```

PROGRAM 56

Q: WRITE A PROGRAM TO FIND GREATEST COMMON DIVISOR USING RECURSIVE FUNCTION.

A:
```c
#include<stdio.h>
int GCD (int, int);
int main ()
{
  int a, b, c;
  printf ("Please Enter the two numbers :\n");
  scanf ("%d%d", &a, &b);
  c = GCD (a, b);
  printf ("GCD of two numbers is=%d\n\n", c);
}

int GCD (int x, int y)
{
  if (x > y)
    GCD (x - y, y);
  if (x < y)
    GCD (x, y - x);
  if (x == y)
    return (y);
}
```

OUTPUT:

```
Please Enter the two numbers :
15
20
GCD of two numbers is=5
```

PROGRAM 57

Q: WRITE A PROGRAM TO FIND FACTORIAL OF NUMBER USING A
RECURSIVE FUNCTION.

A:
```c
#include<stdio.h>
#include<conio.h>
int factorial(int);
int fact=1;
void main()
{
    int num,result;
    printf("Enter the number=");
    scanf("%d",&num);
    result=factorial(num);
    printf("Factorial is=%d\n\n",result);
}
    int factorial(int n)
{
    if(n==1)
    return (1);
    else
    fact=n*factorial(n-1);
    return (fact);
}
```

OUTPUT:

```
Enter the number=5
Factorial is=120
```

PROGRAM 58

Q: WRITE A PROGRAM TO PRINT POWER OF NUMBER USING RECURSIVE FUNCTION.

A:
```c
#include<stdio.h>
int power(int, int);

int main()
{
    int i,j;
    printf("Enter base : ");
    scanf("%d",&i);
    printf("Enter power : ");
    scanf("%d",&j);
    printf("Anser is = %d\n",power(i,j));
    return 0;
}

int power(int i,int j)
{
    if(j==1)
        return i;
    return (i*power(i,j-1));
}
```

OUTPUT:

```
Enter base : 5
Enter power : 2
Anser is = 25
Program ended with exit code: 0
```

PROGRAM 59

Q: WRITE A PROGRAM TO PRINT THE nth TERM OF FIBONACCI SERIES USING RECURSIVE FUNCTION.

A:
```c
#include<stdio.h>
int fib(int);

int main()
{
    int n;
    printf("Type any value : ");
    scanf("%d",&n);
    printf("\nNth value: %d\n",fib(n));
    return 0;
}

int fib(int n)
{
    if(n<=1)
        return n;
    return(fib(n-1)+fib(n-2));
}
```

OUTPUT:

```
Type any value : 6

Nth value: 8
Program ended with exit code: 0
```

PROGRAM 60

Q: WRITE A PROGRAM TO PRINT REVERSE OF A NUMBER USING RECURSIVE FUNCTION.

A:
```c
#include<stdio.h>
int reverse(int, int);

int main()
{
    int N;
    printf("Type a value : ");
    scanf("%d",&N);
    printf("Reverse is : %d\n",reverse(N,0));
    return 0;
}

int reverse(int a, int b)
{
    if(a > 0)
        return reverse(a/10,(b*10)+(a%10));
    return b;
}
```

OUTPUT:

```
Type a value : 12345
Reverse is : 54321
Program ended with exit code: 0
```

126

PROGRAM 61

Q: WRITE A PROGRAM TO PRINT SUM OF DIGITS USING RECURSIVE FUNCTION.

A:

```c
#include<stdio.h>
int sum(int);

int main()
{
    int num;
    printf("Type any number : ");
    scanf("%d",&num);
    printf("Sum of digit: %d\n",sum(num));
    return 0;
}

int sum(int num)
{
    if(num<1)
        return 0;
    return(num%10+sum(num/10));
}
```

OUTPUT:

```
Type any number : 4352
Sum of digit: 14
Program ended with exit code: 0
```

PROGRAM 62

Q: WRITE A PROGRAM TO PRINT TO CONVERT DECIMAL TO BINARY USING RECURSIVE FUNCTION.

A:
```c
#include<stdio.h>
void binary(long);
int main()
{
    long num;
    printf("Type a number : ");
    scanf("%ld",&num);
    binary(num);
    printf("\n");
    return 0;
}

void binary(long num)
{
    if(num>1)
        binary(num/2);
    printf("%ld",num%2);
}
```

OUTPUT:

```
Type a number : 125.56
1111101
Program ended with exit code: 0
```

PROGRAM 63

Q: WRITE A PROGRAM TO FIND THE LENGTH OF A STRING (USING BUILT IN FUNCTION).

A:
```c
#include<stdio.h>

int main()
{
    char str[10];
    int value;
    printf("Enter your name :\n");
    gets(str);                          //fgets is a better option.
    value = strlen(str);
    printf("The length of string is :%d\n",value);

    return 0;

}
```

OUTPUT:

```
Enter your name :
warning: this program uses gets(), which is unsafe.
ansh
The length of string is :4
Program ended with exit code: 0
```

PROGRAM 64

Q: WRITE A PROGRAM TO PRINT LENGTH OF A STRING WITHOUT USING BUILT IN FUNCTION.

A:
```c
#include<stdio.h>

int main()
{
    char str[30];
    int i;
    printf("Enter your name :\n");
    gets(str);
    for(i=0;str[i]!='\0';)
    {
        i++;
    }
    printf("The length of string is :%d\n",i);

    return 0;

}
```

OUTPUT:

```
Enter your name :
warning: this program uses gets(), which is unsafe.
harrypotter
The length of string is :11
Program ended with exit code: 0
```

PROGRAM 65

Q: WRITE A PROGRAM TO COMPARE TWO STRINGS USING BUILT IN FUNCTION.

A:
```c
#include<stdio.h>

int main()
{
    char str1[30],str2[30];
    int value;
    printf("Enter first string:\n");
    gets(str1);
    printf("Enter second string:\n");
    gets(str2);
    value=strcmp(str1,str2);
    if(value==0)
        printf("Both strings are equal\n");
    else if(value>1)
        printf("First string is bigger\n");
    else if(value<1)
        printf("Second string is bigger\n");
    return 0;

}
```

OUTPUT:

```
Enter first string:
warning: this program uses gets(), which is unsafe.
Harry
Enter second string:
Harry
Both strings are equal
Program ended with exit code: 0
```

PROGRAM 66

Q: WRITE A PROGRAM TO COPY ONE STRING TO ANOTHER USING BUILT IN FUNCTION.

A:
```c
#include<stdio.h>

int main()
{
    char str1[30],str2[30];
    printf("Enter first string:\n");
    gets(str1);
    strcpy(str2, str1);
    printf("Copied string is: %s\n",str2);

    return 0;

}
```

OUTPUT:

```
Enter first string:
warning: this program uses gets(), which is unsafe.
Chandler
Copied string is: Chandler
Program ended with exit code: 0
```

PROGRAM 67

Q: WRITE A PROGRAM TO COPY ONE STRING TO ANOTHER WITHOUT USING BUILT IN FUNCTION.

A:

```c
#include<stdio.h>

int main()
{
    char str1[30],str2[30];
    int i=0;
    printf("Enter first string:\n");
    gets(str1);
    while(str1[i]!='\0')
    {
        str2[i]=str1[i];
        i++;
    }
    str2[i]='\0';
    printf("Copied string is: %s\n",str2);
    return 0;

}
```

OUTPUT:

```
Enter first string:
warning: this program uses gets(), which is unsafe.
Batman
Copied string is: Batman
Program ended with exit code: 0
```

133

PROGRAM 68

Q: WRITE A PROGRAM TO CONVERT THE STRING INTO LOWER CASE USING BUILT IN FUNCTION.

A:
```c
#include<stdio.h>

int main()
{
    char str1[30];
    printf("Enter first string:\n");
    gets(str1);
    strlwr(str1);
    printf("MODIFIED STRING:%s\n",str1);

    return 0;

}
```

OUTPUT:

```
Enter first string:
warning: this program uses gets(), which is unsafe.
INFINITYWARS
MODIFIED STRING: infinitywars
Program ended with exit code: 0
```

PROGRAM 69

Q: WRITE A PROGRAM TO CONVERT A STRING INTO UPPER CASE USING BUILT IN FUNCTION.

A:
```c
#include<stdio.h>
int main()
{
    char str1[30];
    printf("Enter first string:\n");
    gets(str1);
    strupr(str1),
    printf("MODIFIED STRING:%s\n",str1);

    return 0;

}
```

OUTPUT:

```
Enter first string:
warning: this program uses gets(), which is unsafe.
ironman
MODIFIED STRING: IRONMAN
Program ended with exit code: 0
```

135

PROGRAM 70

Q: WRITE A PROGRAM TO CONVERT UPPER CASE TO LOWER CASE AND LOWER CASE TO UPPER CASE IN A STRING.

A:
```c
#include<stdio.h>
int main()
{
    char str1[30];
    int i=0;
    printf("Enter first string:\n");
    gets(str1);
    while(str1[i]!='\0')
    {
        if(str1[i]>='a'&&str1[i]<='z')
            str1[i]=str1[i]-32;
        else if(str1[i]>='A'&&str1[i]<='Z')
            str1[i]=str1[i]+32;
    i++;
    }
    printf("MODIFIED STRING: %s\n",str1);

    return 0;
}
```

OUTPUT:

```
Enter first string:
warning: this program uses gets(), which is unsafe.
TONYstark
MODIFIED STRING: tonySTARK
Program ended with exit code: 0
```

PROGRAM 71

Q: WRITE A PROGRAM TO REVERSE A STRING USING BUILT IN FUNCTION.

A:
```c
#include<stdio.h>

int main()
{
    char str1[30];
    printf("Enter first string:\n");
    gets(str1);

    strrev(str1);

    printf("The Reversed string is :%s\n",str1);
    return 0;

}
```

OUTPUT:

```
Enter first string:
warning: this program uses gets(), which is unsafe.
GNIZAMA
The Reversed string is :AMAZING
Program ended with exit code: 0
```

PROGRAM 72

Q: WRITE A PROGRAM TO REVERSE A STRING WITHOUT USING BUILT IN FUNCTION.

A:
```c
#include<stdio.h>
int main()
{
    char str1[30];
    int i=0;
    printf("Enter first string:\n");
    gets(str1);
    while(str1[i]!='\0')
    {
        i++;
    }
    i--;
    printf("The Reversed string is :");
    while(i>=0)
    {
        printf("%c",str1[i]);
        i--;
    }
    printf("\n");
    return 0;
}
```

OUTPUT:

```
Enter first string:
warning: this program uses gets(), which is unsafe.
REVERSEME
The Reversed string is :EMESREVER
Program ended with exit code: 0
```

PROGRAM 73

Q: WRITE A PROGRAM TO CONCATENATE TWO STRINGS USING BUILT IN FUNCTION.

A:
```c
#include<stdio.h>

int main()
{
    char str1[30],str2[30];
    printf("Enter first string:\n");
    gets(str1);
    printf("Enter two strings:\n");
    gets(str2);
    strcat(str1, str2);
    printf("Concatenated string is :%s\n",str1);

    return 0;

}
```

OUTPUT:

```
Enter first string:
warning: this program uses gets(), which is unsafe.
Harvey
Enter two strings:
Specter
Concatenated string is :HarveySpecter
Program ended with exit code: 0
```

PROGRAM 74

Q: WRITE A PROGRAM TO CONCATENATE TWO STRINGS WITHOUT USING BUILT IN FUNCTION.

A:
```c
#include <stdio.h>
int main()
{
    char str1[100], str2[100];
    int i, j;
    printf("Enter first string: ");
    scanf("%s", str1);
    printf("Enter second string: ");
    scanf("%s", str2);
    for(i = 0; str1[i] != '\0'; ++i);
    for(j = 0; str2[j] != '\0'; ++j, ++i)
    {
        str1[i] = str2[j];
    }
    str1[i] = '\0';
    printf("After concatenation: %s\n", str1);
    return 0;
}
```

OUTPUT:

```
Enter first string: Wonder
Enter second string: Woman
After concatenation: WonderWoman
Program ended with exit code: 0
```

PROGRAM 75

Q: WRITE A PROGRAM TO CALCULATE THE OCCURRENCE OF CHARACTER IN A STRING.

A:
```c
#include <stdio.h>
int main()
{
    char str1[100],c;
    int i,count=0;
    printf("Enter first string:\n");
    gets(str1);
    printf("Enter the character:");
    scanf("%c",&c);
    for(i = 0; str1[i] != '\0'; i++)
    {
        if(c==str1[i])
            count++;
    }
    printf("Occurrence is :%d\n",count);

    return 0;
}
```

OUTPUT:

```
Enter first string:
warning: this program uses gets(), which is unsafe.
MISSISSIPPI
Enter the character:S
Occurrence is :4
Program ended with exit code: 0
```

PROGRAM 76

Q: WRITE A PROGRAM TO PRINT MAXIMUM NUMBER IN AN ARRAY.

A:
```c
#include<stdio.h>
int main()
{
    int arr[10],i,max=0;
    printf("Enter 10 value:\n");
    for(i=0;i<10;i++)
    {
        scanf("%d",&arr[i]);
    }
    max=arr[0];
    for(i=0;i<10;i++)
    {
        if(max<arr[i])
            max=arr[i];
    }
    printf("Maximum :%d\n",max);
    return 0;
}
```

OUTPUT:

```
Enter 10 value:
1
9
2
8
3
7
4
6
5
10
Maximum :10
Program ended with exit code: 0
```

PROGRAM 77

Q: WRITE A PROGRAM TO PRINT THE MINIMUM NUMBER IN AN ARRAY.

A:
```c
#include<stdio.h>
int main()
{
    int arr[10],i,min=0;
    printf("Enter 10 value:\n");
    for(i=0;i<10;i++)
    {
        scanf("%d",&arr[i]);
    }
    min=arr[0];
    for(i=0;i<10;i++)
    {
        if(min>arr[i])
            min=arr[i];
    }
    printf("Minimum :%d\n",min);
    return 0;
}
```

OUTPUT:

```
Enter 10 value:
2
3
4
5
6
7
1
8
9
10
Minimum :1
Program ended with exit code: 0
```

143

PROGRAM 78

Q: WRITE A PROGRAM TO REVERSE AN INTEGER ARRAY.

A:
```c
#include<stdio.h>
int main()
{
    int arr[10],i;
    printf("Enter 10 value:\n");
    for(i=0;i<10;i++)
    {
        scanf(" %d",&arr[i]);
    }
    printf("Reversed array is:\n");
    for(i=9;i>=0;i--)
    {
        printf("%d ",arr[i]);
    }
    printf("\n");
    return 0;
}
```

OUTPUT:

```
Enter 10 value:
1 2 3 4 5 6 7 8 9 10
Reversed array is:
10 9 8 7 6 5 4 3 2 1
Program ended with exit code: 0
```

PROGRAM 79

Q: WRITE A PROGRAM TO FIND THE SUM AND AVERAGE OF AN ARRAY.

A:
```c
#include<stdio.h>
int main()
{
    int arr[10],i,sum=0;
    printf("Enter 10 value:\n");
    for(i=0;i<10;i++)
    {
        scanf(" %d",&arr[i]);
    }
    for(i=0;i<10;i++)
    {
        sum=sum+arr[i];
    }
    printf("SUM is: %d\n",sum);
    printf("Average is :%.2f\n",sum/10.0);
    //10 is the number of elements in array.
    return 0;
}
```

OUTPUT:

```
Enter 10 value:
3
3
3
3
3
3
3
3
3
3
SUM is: 30
Average is :3.00
Program ended with exit code: 0
```

PROGRAM 80

Q: WRITE A PROGRAM TO SORT ELEMENTS IN AN ARRAY (BUBBLE SORT).

A:
```c
#include<stdio.h>
int main()
{
    int arr[100],i,temp=0,n,j;
    printf("Enter number of terms:\n");
    scanf("%d",&n);
    printf("Array is :");
    for(i=0;i<n;i++)
    {
        scanf("%d",&arr[i]);
    }
    for(i=0;i<n;i++)
    {
        for(j=0;j<n-i-1;j++)
        {
            if(arr[j]>arr[j+1])
            {
                temp=arr[j];
                arr[j]=arr[j+1];
                arr[j+1]=temp;
            }
        }
    }
    printf("Sorted array:");
    for(i=0;i<n;i++)
    {
        printf("%d ",arr[i]);
    }
    printf("\n");
    return 0;
}
```

OUTPUT:

```
Enter number of terms:
9
Array is :9 8 7 6 5 4 3 2 1
Sorted array:1 2 3 4 5 6 7 8 9
Program ended with exit code: 0
```

PROGRAM 81

Q: WRITE A PROGRAM TO SORT AN ARRAY USING INSERTION SORT.

A:
```c
#include<stdio.h>
int main()
{
    int arr[100], i, temp, n, j;
    printf("Enter number of terms:\n");
    scanf("%d",&n);
    printf("Array is :");
    for(i=0;i<n;i++)
    {
        scanf("%d",&arr[i]);
    }
    for(i=1;i<=n-1;i++)
    {
        j=i;
        while(j>0&&arr[j-1]> arr[j])
        {
            temp=arr[j];
            arr[j]=arr[j-1];
            arr[j-1]=temp;
            j--;
        }
    }
    printf("Sorted array:");
    for(i=0;i<=n-1;i++)
    {
        printf("%d ",arr[i]);
    }
    printf("\n");
    return 0;
}
```

OUTPUT:

```
Enter number of terms:
9
Array is :9 8 7 6 5 4 3 2 1
Sorted array:1 2 3 4 5 6 7 8 9
Program ended with exit code: 0
```

PROGRAM 82

Q: WRITE A PROGRAM TO SORT AN ARRAY USING SELECTION SORT.
A:
```c
#include<stdio.h>
int main()
{
    int arr[100],i,temp,n,j,k;
    printf("Enter number of terms:\n");
    scanf("%d",&n);
    printf("Array is :");
    for(i=0;i<n;i++)
    {
        scanf("%d",&arr[i]);
    }
    for(i=0;i<n;i++)
    {
        k=i;
        for(j=i; j<n ;j++)
        {
            if(arr[k] > arr[j])
                k=j;
        }
        if(k!=i)
        {
            temp=arr[k];
            arr[k]=arr[i];
            arr[i]=temp;
        }
    }
    printf("Sorted array:");
    for(i=0;i<n;i++)
    {
        printf("%d ",arr[i]);
    }
    printf("\n");
    return 0;
}
```

OUTPUT:

```
Enter number of terms:
9
Array is :9 8 6 7 5 3 4 2 1
Sorted array:1 2 3 4 5 6 7 8 9
Program ended with exit code: 0
```

PROGRAM 83

Q: WRITE A PROGRAM TO SEARCH AN ELEMENT IN AN ARRAY USING LINEAR SEARCH.

A:
```c
#include<stdio.h>
int main()
{
    int arr[20],i,n,val,index;
    printf("Enter number of values: ");
    scanf("%d",&n);
    for(i=0;i<n;i++)
    {
        scanf("%d",&arr[i]);
    }
    index=-2; // anything below zero.
    printf("\nEnter a value to be searched: ");
    scanf("%d",&val);
    for(i=0;i<n;i++)
    {
        if(val==arr[i])
        {
            index=i;
            break;
        }
    }
    if(index>=0)
        printf("\nValue found in Array at %dth location\n",index+1);
    else
        printf("\nValue not found in Array\n");

    return 0;

}
```

OUTPUT:

```
Enter number of values: 10
1
2
3
6
7
8
9
0
4
5

Enter a value to be searched: 6

Value found in Array at 4th location
Program ended with exit code: 0
```

PROGRAM 84

Q: WRITE A PROGRAM TO SEARCH AN ELEMENT IN AN ARRAY USING BINARY SEARCH METHOD.

A:
```c
#include<stdio.h>
int main()
{
    int arr[20], i, max, min, mid, val, n, index;
    printf("Enter number of elements:");
    scanf("%d",&n);
    printf("\nPlease enter %d values in ascending order:\n",n);
    for(i=0;i<n;i++)
    {
        scanf("%d",&arr[i]);
    }
    printf("\nEnter a value to be searched: ");
    scanf("%d",&val);
    max= n-1;
    min= 0;
    index= -2;
    while(min<=max)
    {
        mid=(min + max)/2;
        if(val==arr[mid])
        {
            index=mid;
            break;
        }
        if(arr[mid]>val)
            max=mid-1;
        else
            min=mid+1;
    }
    if(index>=0)
        printf("\nValue found in Array at %dth location\n",index+1);
    else
        printf("\nValue not found in Array\n");
    return 0;
}
```

154

OUTPUT:

```
Enter number of elements:10

Please enter 10 values in ascending order:
1
3
5
7
9
11
13
15
17
19

Enter a value to be searched: 11

Value found in Array at 6th location
Program ended with exit code: 0
```

PROGRAM 85

Q: WRITE A PROGRAM TO ADD TWO MATRICES USING TWO DIMENSIONAL ARRAY.

A:

```c
#include<stdio.h>
int main()
{   int mat1[10][10],mat2[10][10],mat3[10][10],i, j, n;
    printf("Enter value of n in n*n matrix:");
    scanf("%d",&n);
    printf("\nEnter %d elements of first matrix:\n",n*n);
    for(i=0;i<n;i++)
    {
        for(j=0;j<n;j++)
        {
            scanf("%d",&mat1[i][j]);
        }
    }
    printf("\nEnter %d elements of second matrix:\n",n*n);
    for(i=0;i<n;i++)
    {
        for(j=0;j<n;j++)
        {
            scanf("%d",&mat2[i][j]);
        }
    }
    printf("Sum of above two matrices is:\n");
    for(i=0;i<n;i++)
    {
        for(j=0;j<n;j++)
        {
            mat3[i][j]=mat1[i][j]+mat2[i][j];
            printf("%d ",mat3[i][j]);
            if(j==2)                  // This if statement is optional.
            {
                printf("\n");
            }
        }
    }
    return 0;
}
```

OUTPUT:

```
Enter value of n in n*n matrix:3

Enter 9 elements of first matrix:
1 2 3
4 5 6
7 8 9

Enter 9 elements of second matrix:
9 8 7
6 5 4
3 2 1
Sum of above two matrices is:
10 10 10
10 10 10
10 10 10
Program ended with exit code: 0
```

PROGRAM 86

Q:WRITE A PROGRAM TO SUBTRACT TWO MATRICES USING 2D ARRAY
A:

```c
#include<stdio.h>
int main()
{
    int mat1[10][10],mat2[10][10],mat3[10][10],i,j,n;
    printf("Enter value of n in n*n matrix:");
    scanf("%d",&n);
    printf("\nEnter %d elements of first matrix:\n",n*n);
    for(i=0;i<n;i++)
    {
        for(j=0;j<n;j++)
        {
            scanf("%d",&mat1[i][j]);
        }
    }
    printf("\nEnter %d elements of second matrix:\n",n*n);
    for(i=0;i<n;i++)
    {
        for(j=0;j<n;j++)
        {
            scanf("%d",&mat2[i][j]);
        }
    }
    printf("Subtraction of above two matrices is:\n");
    for(i=0;i<n;i++)
    {
        for(j=0;j<n;j++)
        {
            mat3[i][j]=mat1[i][j]-mat2[i][j];
            printf("%d ",mat3[i][j]);
            if(j==2)                        // This if statement is optional.
            {
                printf("\n");
            }
        }
    }
    return 0;
}
```

OUTPUT:

```
Enter value of n in n*n matrix:3

Enter 9 elements of first matrix:
11 12 13
14 15 16
17 18 19

Enter 9 elements of second matrix:
1 2 3
4 5 6
7 8 9
Subtraction of above two matrices is:
10 10 10
10 10 10
10 10 10
Program ended with exit code: 0
```

PROGRAM 87

Q: WRITE A PROGRAM TO TRANSPOSE TWO MATRICES.

A:
```c
#include<stdio.h>
int main()
{
    int mat1[10][10],mat2[10][10],i, j, n;
    printf("Enter value of n in n*n matrix:");
    scanf("%d",&n);
    printf("\nEnter %d elements of matrix:\n",n*n);
    for(i=0;i<n;i++)
    {
        for(j=0;j<n;j++)
        {
            scanf("%d",&mat1[i][j]);
        }
    }
    printf("\n\nTranspose of above matrix is:\n");
    for(i=0;i<n;i++)
    {
        for(j=0;j<n;j++)
        {
            mat2[i][j]=mat1[j][i];
            printf("%d ",mat2[i][j]);
            if(j==2)                    // This if statement is optional.
            {
                printf("\n");
            }
        }
    }

    return 0;
}
```

OUTPUT:

```
Enter value of n in n*n matrix: 3

Enter 9 elements of matrix:
1 2 3
4 5 6
7 8 9


Transpose of above matrix is:
1 4 7
2 5 8
3 6 9
Program ended with exit code: 0
```

PROGRAM 88

Q: WRITE A PROGRAM TO MULTIPLY TWO MATRICES.

A:
```c
#include<stdio.h>
int main()
{
    int mat1[10][10],mat2[10][10],mat3[10][10],i,j,n,k;
    printf("Enter value of n in n*n matrix:");
    scanf("%d",&n);
    printf("\nEnter %d elements of first matrix:\n",n*n);
    for(i=0;i<n;i++)
    {
        for(j=0;j<n;j++)
        {
            scanf("%d",&mat1[i][j]);
        }
    }
    printf("\nEnter %d elements of second matrix:\n",n*n);
    for(i=0;i<n;i++)
    {
        for(j=0;j<n;j++)
        {
            scanf("%d",&mat2[i][j]);
        }
    }
    printf("\nProduct of above two matrices is:\n");
    for(i=0;i<n;i++)
    {
        for(j=0;j<n;j++)
        {
            mat3[i][j]=0;
            for(k=0;k<n;k++)
            {
                mat3[i][j]=mat3[i][j]+mat1[i][k]*mat2[k][j];
            }
            printf("%d ",mat3[i][j]);
            if(j==2)        // This if statement is optional.
            {
```

```c
        printf("\n");
      }
    }
  }
  return 0;
}
```

OUTPUT:

```
Enter value of n in n*n matrix: 3

Enter 9 elements of first matrix:
2 2 2
2 2 2
2 2 2

Enter 9 elements of second matrix:
2 2 2
2 2 2
2 2 2

Product of above two matrices is:
12 12 12
12 12 12
12 12 12
Program ended with exit code: 0
```

PROGRAM 89

Q: WRITE A PROGRAM TO PRINT THE UPPER TRIANGLE ELEMENTS OF A MATRIX.

A:
```c
#include<stdio.h>
int main()
{
    int mat1[10][10], i , j, n;
    printf("Enter value of n in n*n matrix:");
    scanf("%d",&n);
    printf("\nEnter %d elements of matrix:\n",n*n);
    for(i=0;i<n;i++)
    {
        for(j=0;j<n;j++)
        {
            scanf("%d",&mat1[i][j]);
        }
    }
    printf("\nUpper triangle of matrix is:\n");
    for(i=0;i<n;i++)
    {
        for(j=0;j<n;j++)
        {
            if(j>=i)
                printf("%d ",mat1[i][j]);
            else
                printf("  ");  //double spacing here.
        }
        printf("\n");        //row change or use if statement in inner for loop.
    }
    return 0;
}
```

OUTPUT:

```
Enter value of n in n*n matrix: 3

Enter 9 elements of matrix:
1 2 3
4 5 6
7 8 9

Upper triangle of matrix is:
1 2 3
  5 6
    9
Program ended with exit code: 0
```

PROGRAM 90

Q: WRITE A PROGRAM TO PRINT DIAGONAL ELEMENTS OF A MATRIX.

A:
```c
#include<stdio.h>
int main()
{
    int mat1[10][10],i , j, n;
    printf("Enter value of n in n*n matrix:");
    scanf("%d",&n);
    printf("\nEnter %d elements of matrix:\n",n*n);
    for(i=0;i<n;i++)
    {
        for(j=0; j<n ;j++)
        {
            scanf("%d",&mat1[i][j]);
        }
    }
    printf("\nDiagonal of a matrix is:\n");
    for(i=0;i<n;i++)
    {
        for(j=0; j<n ;j++)
        {
            if(j==i)
                printf("%d ",mat1[i][j]);
            else
                printf("  ");  //double spacing here.
        }
        printf("\n");        //row change or use if statement in inner for loop.
    }

    return 0;
}
```

OUTPUT:

```
Enter value of n in n*n matrix: 3

Enter 9 elements of matrix:
1 2 3
4 5 6
7 8 9

Diagonal of a matrix is:
1
    5
        9
Program ended with exit code: 0
```

PROGRAM 91

Q: WRITE A PROGRAM TO DEMONSTRATE THE USE OF SWITCH CASE USING DO-WHILE LOOP.
A:
```c
#include<stdio.h>
#include<math.h>
int main()
{
    int ch, num;
    printf("*******************!!MENU!!*******************\n\n");
    printf("1.Calculate the square of the number.\n");
    printf("2.Calculate the square root of the number.\n");
    printf("3.Calculate the cube of the number.\n");
    printf("\nEnter the number: ");
    scanf("%d",&num);
    do
    {
        printf("Enter -1 to exit!\n\n");
        printf("Enter your Choice from above: ");
        scanf("%d",&ch);
        switch(ch)
        {
            case 1:
                printf("\nThe Square of the number is= %d\n",num*num);
                break;
            case 2:
                printf("\nThe Square root of the number is= %f\n",sqrt(num));
                break;
            case 3:
                printf("\nThe cube of the number is= %f\n",pow(num,3));
                break;
            default:
                printf("\nThe Number you had given is= %d\n",num);
        }
    }while(ch!=-1);
    return 0;
}
```

OUTPUT:

```
*******************!!MENU!!*******************
1.Calculate the square of the number.
2.Calculate the square root of the number.
3.Calculate the cube of the number.

Enter the number: 9
Enter -1 to exit!

Enter your Choice from above: 1

The Square of the number is= 81
Enter -1 to exit!

Enter your Choice from above: 2

The Square root of the number is= 3.000000
Enter -1 to exit!

Enter your Choice from above: 3

The cube of the number is= 729.000000
Enter -1 to exit!

Enter your Choice from above: -1

The Number you had given is= 9
Program ended with exit code: 0
```

PROGRAM 92

Q: WRITE A PROGRAM TO SWAP TWO VALUES USING CALL BY VALUE.

A:
```
#include<stdio.h>
int SwapVal(int,int);
int main()
{
    int x=10,y=20;
    printf("Before calling function SwapVal x=%d,y=%d\n",x,y);
    SwapVal(x,y);
    printf("\nAfter Calling the function SwapVal c=%d,y=%d\n\n",x,y);
}
int SwapVal(int x,int y)
{ int temp;
    temp=x;
    x=y;
    y=temp;
    printf("\nWithin the function SwapVal x=%d,y=%d\n",x,y);
    return 0;
}
```

OUTPUT:

```
Before calling function SwapVal x=10,y=20

Within the function SwapVal x=20,y=10

After Calling the function SwapVal c=10,y=20

Program ended with exit code: 0
```

PROGRAM 93

Q: WRITE A PROGRAM TO SWAP TWO VALUES USING CALL BY REFERENCE USING POINTER.

A:
```c
#include<stdio.h>
int SwapRef(int*,int*);
int main()
{
    int x=10,y=20;
    printf("\nBefore Calling the function SwapRef c=%d,y=%d\n",x,y);
    SwapRef(&x,&y);
    printf("\nAfter Calling the function SwapRef x=%d,y=%d\n\n",x,y);
}
int SwapRef(int*px,int*py)
{
    int temp;
    temp= *px;
    *px = *py;
    *py = temp;
    printf("\nWithin the function SwapRef x=%d,y=%d\n",*px,*py);
    return 0;
}
```

OUTPUT:

```
Before Calling the function SwapRef c=10,y=20

Within the function SwapRef x=20,y=10

After Calling the function SwapRef x=20,y=10

Program ended with exit code: 0
```

PROGRAM 94

Q: WRITE A PROGRAM TO FIND THE AREA AND PERIMETER OF RECTANGLE BY CALL BY REFERENCE USING POINTERS.

A:
```c
#include<stdio.h>
int periarea(float, float, float *a, float *b);
int main()
{
    float len,br;
    float peri,ar;
    printf("Enter the Length and Breadth of Rectangle in meters:\n");
    scanf("%f%f",&len,&br);
    periarea(len,br,&peri,&ar);
    printf("Perimeter of the Rectangle is= %fmeters\n",peri);
    printf("\nArea of the rectangle is= %fsquare meters\n\n",ar);
}
int periarea(float length,float breadth,float *perimeter,float *area)
{
    *perimeter= 2*(length+breadth);
    *area= length*breadth;
    return 0;
}
```

OUTPUT:

```
Enter the Length and Breadth of Rectangle in meters:
10
20
Perimeter of the Rectangle is= 60.000000meters

Area of the rectangle is= 200.000000square meters

Program ended with exit code: 0
```

PROGRAM 95

Q: WRITE A PROGRAM TO PRINT MARK SHEET OF STUDENTS IN A CLASS BY USING STRUCTURE ARRAY.

A:
```c
#include<stdio.h>
struct marksheet{
    char name[20];
    char regno[16];
    int marks[8];
    char grade[8];
} s[60];

int main()
{
    char sub[7]
[20]={"Adv.Maths","Physics","Chemistry","Computer","Electrical","Aptitude","English"};
    char subcode[7]
[10]={"MAT1","PHY2","CHEM3","COMP4","EC5","APT6","ENG7"};
    int i,j;
    for(i=0;i<=0;i++)
    {
        printf("Name of the student=\n");
        scanf("%s",s[i].name);
        printf("Registration number=\n");
        scanf("%s",s[i].regno);
        for( j=0;j<7;j++)
        { printf("Enter the marks in %s (%s)=",sub[j],subcode[j]);
            scanf("%d",&s[i].marks[j]);
        }
    }
    for(i=0;i<=0;i++)
    {
        for(j=0;j<=7;j++)
        {
            if(s[i].marks[j]>=95)
                s[i].grade[j]='O';
            else if(s[i].marks[j]<95&&s[i].marks[j]>=90)
                s[i].grade[j]='A';
            else if(s[i].marks[j]<90&&s[i].marks[j]>=85)
                s[i].grade[j]='A';
            else if(s[i].marks[j]<85&&s[i].marks[j]>=75)
                s[i].grade[j]='B';
```

```c
        else if(s[i].marks[j]<75&&s[i].marks[j]>=65)
            s[i].grade[j]='B';
        else  if(s[i].marks[j]<65&&s[i].marks[j]>=55)
            s[i].grade[j]='C';
        else if(s[i].marks[j]<55&&s[i].marks[j]>=50)
            s[i].grade[j]='D';
        else
            s[i].grade[j]='F';
        }
    }
    for(i=0;i<=0;i++)
    {
        printf("\n\n");
        printf("-----------------------------------------------------------------
\n");
        printf("\t\t\t\tSELF LEARNING INSTITUTE OF TECHNOLOGY");
        printf("\n\t\t\t\t\t\tDELHI");
        printf("\n-----------------------------------------------------------------
");
        printf("\nName=%s",s[i].name);
        printf("\nReg No.=%s",s[i].regno);

printf("\n---------------------------------------------------------------------");
        printf("\nSemester\tSubject\t\tSubject Code\t\tMarks   Grade");

printf("\n---------------------------------------------------------------------");
        for(j=0;j<7;j++)
        {
            printf("\n");
            printf(" 2\t\t%s\t\t\t%s\t\t\t%d\t\t%c",sub[j],subcode[j],s[i].marks[j],s[i].grade[j]);

        }
    }
        printf("\n---------------------------------------------------------------------");
        printf("\n---------------------------------------------------------------------\n");
    return 0;
}
```

OUTPUT:

```
Name of the student=
Albert
Registration number=
180499
Enter the marks in Adv.Maths (MAT1)=100
Enter the marks in Physics (PHY2)=95
Enter the marks in Chemistry (CHEM3)=90
Enter the marks in Computer (COMP4)=90
Enter the marks in Electrical (EC5)=85
Enter the marks in Aptitude (APT6)=80
Enter the marks in English (ENG7)=92


--------------------------------------------------------
            SELF LEARNING INSTITUTE OF TECHNOLOGY
                         DELHI
--------------------------------------------------------
Name=Albert
Reg No.=180499
--------------------------------------------------------
Semester   Subject        Subject Code      Marks    Grade
--------------------------------------------------------
   2       Adv.Maths      MAT1              100      O
   2       Physics        PHY2              95       O
   2       Chemistry      CHEM3             90       A
   2       Computer       COMP4             90       A
   2       Electrical     EC5               85       A
   2       Aptitude       APT6              80       B
   2       English        ENG7              92       A
--------------------------------------------------------

--------------------------------------------------------
Program ended with exit code: 0
```

PROGRAM 96

Q: WRITE A PROGRAM TO PRINT THE SUM OF COMPLEX NUMBERS IN THE FORM (a+ib) USING STRUCTURES.

A:
```c
#include<stdio.h>
struct complex
{ int real;
    int img;
}a1,a2,a3;
int main()
{
    printf("Enter the real and imaginary part of first complex number:\n");
    scanf("%d%d",&a1.real,&a1.img);
    printf("Enter the real and imaginary part of second complex number:\n");
    scanf("%d%d",&a2.real,&a2.img);
    a3.real=a1.real+a2.real;
    a3.img=a1.img+a2.img;
    printf("\nZ = %d + i%d",a1.real,a1.img);
    printf("\nW = %d + i%d",a2.real,a2.img);
    printf("\nSum of the above Complex Number is:");
    printf("\nZ + W = %d + i%d\n",a3.real,a3.img);
    return 0;
}
```

OUTPUT:

```
Enter the real and imaginary part of first complex number:
4
6
Enter the real and imaginary part of second complex number:
10
20

Z = 4 + i6
W = 10 + i20
Sum of the above Complex Number is:
Z + W = 14 + i26
Program ended with exit code: 0
```

PROGRAM 97

Q: WRITE A PROGRAM TO CALCULATE THE MEAN, VARIANCE AND STANDARD DEVIATION.

A:
```c
#include<stdio.h>
int main()
{
    float variance,stdev, avg,sum2=0,sum=0;
    int arr[10],n,i;
    printf("Enter number of terms : ");
    scanf("%d",&n);
    printf("\n\nEnter Elements:\n");
    for(i=0;i<n;i++)
    {
        scanf(" %d",&arr[i]);
    }
    for(i=0;i<n;i++)
    {
        sum=sum+arr[i];
    }
    avg= sum/n;
    for(i=0;i<n;i++)
    {
        sum2=sum2 + pow(arr[i]-avg,2);
    }
    variance=sum2/n;
    stdev= sqrt(variance);
    printf("\nTHE AVERAGE IS: %.2f",avg);
    printf("\nTHE VARIANCE IS: %.2f",variance);
    printf("\nTHE STANDARD DEVIATION IS: %.2f\n\n",stdev);
    return 0;
}
```

OUTPUT:

```
Enter number of terms : 5

Enter Elements:
34
88
32
12
10

THE AVERAGE IS: 35.20
THE VARIANCE IS: 794.56
THE STANDARD DEVIATION IS: 28.19

Program ended with exit code: 0
```

PROGRAM 98

Q: WRITE A PROGRAM TO SORT NAMES IN ALPHABETICAL ORDER.

A:
```c
#include<stdio.h>
#include<string.h>
int main()
{

    char name[10][8], tempname[10][8], temp[8];
    int i, j, n;
    printf("Enter number of names: \n");
    scanf("%d", &n);
    printf("\nEnter %d names:\n",n);
    for (i = 0; i < n; i++)
    {
        scanf("%s", name[i]);
        strcpy(tempname[i], name[i]);    //copy name to tempname.
    }
    for (i = 0; i < n - 1 ; i++)
    {
        for (j = i + 1; j < n; j++)
        {
            if (strcmp(name[i], name[j]) > 0)   //compare two strings.
            {
                strcpy(temp, name[i]);
                strcpy(name[i], name[j]);
                strcpy(name[j], temp);
            }
        }
    }
    printf("\n**************************************\n");
    printf("\tSorted names\n");
    printf("\n**************************************\n");
    for (i = 0; i < n; i++)
    {
        printf("\t%s\n",name[i]);
    }
    printf("\n**************************************\n");
    return 0;
}
```

OUTPUT:

```
Enter number of names:
5

Enter 5 names:
remote
chair
laptop
table
television

***************************************
       Sorted names

***************************************
       chair
       laptop
       remote
       table
       television

***************************************
Program ended with exit code: 0
```

PROGRAM 99

Q: WRITE A PROGRAM TO FIND NUMBER OF TRAILING ZEROES IN N FACTORIAL.

A:
```c
#include<stdio.h>
int main()
{
    int num,i,count=0;
    long double fact=1;
    printf("Enter the number : ");
    scanf("\n%d",&num);
    for(i=2; i<=num; i++)
    {
        fact = fact*i;
    }
    if(num<0)
        printf("\nInvalid user input.");
    else
        printf("\n%d! = %Lf\n",num, fact);
    for(i=5; num/i !=0 ; i*=5)
    {
        count+=num/i;
    }
    printf("\nThe number of trailing zeroes are: %d\n\n",count);
    return 0;
}
```

OUTPUT:

```
Enter the number : 18

18! = 6402373705728000.000000

The number of trailing zeroes are: 3

Program ended with exit code: 0
```

PROGRAM 100

Q: YOU ARE GIVEN AN ARRAY OF INTEGERS **(POSITIVE AND NEGATIVE)** . FIND A CONTINUOUS SEQUENCE THAT GIVE THE LARGEST SUM. WRITE A PROGRAM TO RETURN THIS LARGEST SUM. (EXAMPLE: input = 1 -7 3 -2 4 -9 5 -4 -6 3 then output=5 (i.e : 3, -2, 4)

A:
```c
#include<stdio.h>
int main()
{
    int sum=0, max=0,n,i, arr[10];
    printf("Enter length of array: ");
    scanf("\n%d",&n);
    printf("\nEnter the numbers:\n");
    printf("\n-----------------------\n");
    for(i=0;i<n;i++)
    {
        scanf("%d",&arr[i]);
    }
    printf("-----------------------\n");
    for(i=0;i<n;i++)
    {
        sum=sum+arr[i];
        if(max<sum)
        {
            max=sum;
        }
        else if(sum<0)
        {
            sum=0;
        }
    }
    printf("\nThe largest sum in this will be: %d\n\n",max);
    return 0;
}
```

OUTPUT:

```
Enter length of array: 10

Enter the numbers:

————————————————————————
1 -7 3 -2 4 -9 5 -4 -6 3
————————————————————————

The largest sum in this will be: 5

Program ended with exit code: 0
```

Made in the USA
San Bernardino, CA
19 November 2019

60155705R00104